Archaeology
of
Clear Creek Canyon

Archaeology
of
Clear Creek Canyon

Joel C. Janetski

with contributions by
Richard K. Talbot, Lane D. Richens, Deborah E.
Newman, James D. Wilde, and Shane A. Baker

Brigham Young University
Provo

Cover: Rock art elements from Clear Creek Canyon

The final version of this report originally prepared for the Utah
Department of Transportation, Salt Lake City, February 1997.

Utah Department of Transportation Contract No. 84-7204
Federal Antiquities Permit No. 92-UT-54624
Utah State Project Authorization No. U-88-BC-048p

Contents

Figures and Table

Contributors

Joel C. Janetski is the principal author of *Archaeology of Clear Creek Canyon* and was one of the principal investigators for the Clear Creek work. He is a professor of anthropology at Brigham Young University where he has directed the archaeological field school for a number of years.

Richard K. Talbot is the manager of the Office of Public Archaeology at Brigham Young University. During the Clear Creek project he and Lane Richens were the primary field supervisors for the duration of the project.

Lane D. Richens is a senior archaeologist with the Office of Public Archaeology. As noted, he directed field work on the project and was responsible for all ceramic analysis.

Deborah E. Newman, a palynologist and botanist in charge of Archaeological Technical Lab at Brigham Young University at the time of the Clear Creek work, was responsible for reconstructing past climates and identifying plants used for food.

James D. Wilde, now the archaeologist for the United States Air Force, managed the Office of Public Archaeology in the 1980s. He supervised the excavations at Sheep Shelter and oversaw the analysis of stone tools on the project.

Shane A. Baker is a staff archaeologist at the Office Public Archaeology and collections manager in the Museum of Peoples and Cultures. His role on the Clear Creek Project was the ordering and reporting of the complex rock art in the canyon.

Acknowledgments

The author and contributors would like to acknowledge the efforts of several individuals who are not mentioned in the text. The contributions and support of J. Kent Taylor, Fishlake National Forest Supervisor and his staff, especially Robert Leonard, Fishlake National Forest archaeologist, during the Clear Creek Canyon Archaeological Project field work and since are simply too many to mention. We thank Bob for his interest and support throughout this massive project. We also fondly acknowledge Asa Nielson who was the director of the Office of Public Archaeology at Brigham Young University during the field phase of the projects whose talents in lobbying for the Fremont Indian State Park were important in the success of that effort.

We express gratitude to Kenny Wintch and Susan Miller of the Utah Department of Transportation for their amazing patience during the completion of the project reports. Finally, we acknowledge the excellent illustrations produced by Jenny Dawn Angona and Tuula Rose, and the computer and editorial skills of Kathy Driggs (Publications Office of the Museum of Peoples and Cultures at BYU) who brought order to this and the other Clear Creek volumes.

Preface

Public monies, both federal and state, provided the funding for archaeological work in advance of the construction of Interstate 70 through Clear Creek Canyon. This short volume written by the excavators highlights findings from excavation and survey, and synthesizes those findings for the interested public. The booklet distills huge amounts of data described in several technical reports on file with the Utah Department of Transportation and other state agencies. Although some Fremont-wide comparative discussion is contained in this volume, it is not intended as a new synthesis of the Fremont.

The Clear Creek Archaeological Project was important for several reasons. Perhaps most significantly, the archaeology was done to obtain broad perspectives on the Fremont. This was done at two different scales or levels: regional and site-specific. At the most general level, the work was canyon-wide in scope, an apporach that required archaeologists to investigate sites throughout the Clear Creek drainage, which made it one of the first regional studies of Fremont settlement in the state. Information from different kinds of sites in different kinds of settings allowed researchers to paint a broader picture of Fremont life than has been possible to date. The second, more site-specific approach, resulted in the first complete excavation of a large village, Five Finger Ridge. This broad, horizontal exposure of a farming community provided a substantive basis for insights into Fremont social life, population levels, and village planning, topics seldom explored in Fremont archaeology.

Construction of Fremont Indian State Park in Clear Creek Canyon is evidence of the importance of the Clear Creek research. All the artifacts recovered during the excavations are now stored in this museum and portions are exhibited in the displays.

"The Red Blanket" Pictograph

Word was received, however, of some Indian material located in Clear Creek Canyon and investigation proved these reports to be correct.

Elmer Smith (1937)

Overview of Five Finger Ridge looking southwest, winter 1984 (note the bulldozed road cutting downward from the saddle area).

1

Clear Creek Canyon Archaeology

Introduction

Clear Creek Canyon lies in south-central Utah a few miles below Richfield. It runs east-west separating the high peaks of the Pavant and Tushar mountains and connecting the upper Sevier Valley to the eastern edge of the Sevier Desert. The canyon is not particularly long nor remarkable, but it gives westbound travelers easy access to the upper Beaver River Valley to the south and Pavant Valley to the north. In its lower reaches, abrupt cliffs of lavender rhyolite bound the narrow flood-plain and document the vulcanism in the deep history of the canyon. Above the cliffs, sage and grass, and a bit higher, juniper and pinyon, cover the slopes and terraces. Higher still are stands of aspen and fir. The upper canyon above Mill Creek is dissected; ragged cliffs and drainages complicate the landscape inviting exploration of the small creeks lined with willows and cottonwoods. Mule deer browse here in the early morning and cottontails are abundant in the thick, high sage along the arroyos. It is a pleasant valley animated by Clear Creek, whose waters have carved the canyon over a thousand millennia.

In 1980 Clear Creek ran free in the lower canyon, winding under the cottonwoods past a few small farmsteads. Beneath the twentieth-century farms along the creek and on knolls overlooking the stream, lay long-forgotten remnants of earlier farms and farmers. These remains tell of several communities that flourished in the canyon a thousand years ago. Called the Fremont by archaeologists, the ancient farmers used the canyons for hundreds of years, and then, for reasons only hinted at in their discard, abandoned their homes and fields. Centuries of wind, rain, and snow eroded and smoothed the adobe walls of the granaries and filled in the depressions left by collapsed houses. Grass and sage flourished on the hill slopes, which helped to hold tools, pottery sherds, and other debris

3

in place. The immutable but abundant rock art decorating the cliff walls enliven the scene for travelers and signal a rich, but poorly known past. Clear Creek Canyon's history is there, etched on the cliffs and buried in the deep soils along the stream.

Today Interstate 70, twin ribbons of concrete and steel, hurries westbound travelers through and out of the canyon to connect with north or southbound Interstate 15. Because of the highway construction, the history of the canyon is now better known. Well before the highway was built, archaeologists began to explore the canyon systematically. This work, required by federal law, was done in advance of the construction of this important link in the Interstate highway system. Many locals knew of the canyon's abundant rock art, and early archaeologists explored the small cave now known as Cave of 100 Hands. But the new, more intensive inspections of the landscape found more sites and several appeared to contain evidence of ancient houses. Since a number of these sites were to be destroyed by the highway, archaeologists from the Utah Division of State History excavated two sites in the canyon in 1979 and 1981: Workshop Knoll overlooking Mill Creek on the south side of the canyon and Lott's Farm along the Creek in the lower canyon. In the winter of 1983, the Office of Public Archaeology (OPA) at Brigham Young University (BYU) began excavations at Icicle Bench at the mouth of Clear Creek Canyon.

The size of the project changed dramatically when a resident of Monroe, Utah, told the archaeologists of a site up the canyon that was also being disturbed by the highway work. His directions led BYU researchers to a large knoll littered with pottery and pocked with depressions of ancient houses. Excavations here uncovered an extensive Fremont village, dubbed Five Finger Ridge by the archaeologists. It is the largest Fremont site excavated to date in the state of Utah, and the first village site ever exposed completely in the history of Fremont archaeology.

In the weeks following the discovery of Five Finger Ridge, a massive, cooperative project was organized to learn more about the history of this small portion of the state. Brigham Young University, Weber State University, the U.S. Forest Service, Utah Division of State History, and the Paiute Indian Tribe of Utah conceptualized and implemented a regional project, focused on the farming or Fremont period. A series of surveys examined selected portions of the uplands as well as the creek bottom for human use and documented the myriad rock art panels— some hidden, some highly visible—scattered along the canyon cliffs.

Test excavations were planned and carried out at sheltered sites and larger village sites in the canyon. This booklet describes the research project and summarizes and interprets sites and material remains that were discovered. A multivolume report (see Additional Readings) detailing the findings was submitted to the Utah Department of Transportation.

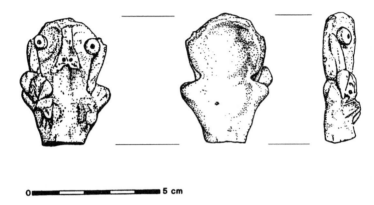

0 ▬▬▬▬▬▬▬ 5 cm

Clay figurine from the floor of Structure Five, Icicle Bench, Utah.

The Fremont drainage proved to be the seat of a distinctive culture . . . characterized by cave sites with a slab cist architecture . . .; a distinctive unpainted black or gray pottery; by the exclusive use of a unique type of moccasin; by a cult of unbaked clay figurines . . .; by abundant pictographs of distinctive types . . .

Noel Morss (1931)

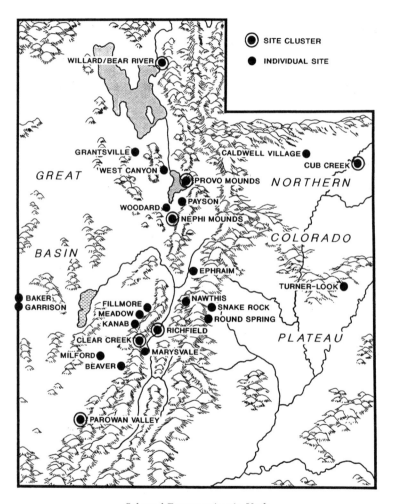

Selected Fremont sites in Utah.

What Was the Fremont Culture?

Fremont is a label archaeologists use to refer to a time as well as a range of lifeways that persisted for several hundred years throughout Utah and neighboring states north of the Colorado and Virgin Rivers. The Fremont term comes from the Fremont River where archaeologist Noel Morss of the Peabody Museum at Harvard University worked in the 1920s. Based on his excavations along this river in and near present-day Capital Reef National Park, he defined the Fremont as farmers similar to the Anasazi farther south, but, as he noted in the above quotation, distinctive in a number of ways. Morss was not the first to excavate at what are now known as Fremont sites. Fremont archaeology began well before the turn of the century. As early as the 1870s, archaeologists explored highly visible mounds in the valleys along the eastern Great Basin rim as well as the Colorado Plateau to the east. In 1892 Henry Montgomery of the University of Utah excavated mounds at Nephi, explored the extensive ruins at Paragonah, and probed the deep and fascinating Nine Mile Canyon. He finally concluded those ruins were made by the same people who left the many cliff dwellings in Arizona and Colorado. He was greatly impressed by the masonry towers built high on the cliffs in Nine Mile Canyon and decided these were "military posts" or "watch stations" of "a great nation whose headquarters were probably in Mexico" (see Montgomery 1894 in Additional Readings). Neil Judd, Julian Steward, and other archaeologists working in the 1910s, 1920s, and 1930s excavated Fremont ruins along the Wasatch Front and were taken by the similarities between Fremont and Anasazi sites and artifacts, especially ceramics and architecture. Because of these similarities, Fremont remains were often referred to as "Puebloan" (because the Anasazi often lived in pueblos similar to those of the Hopi) and the pithouses were called kivas. Although the Puebloan label has long since been dropped, most recognize that occasional influence and interaction must have occurred between the Fremont and Anasazi.

Research on the Fremont continued during the 1950s, 1960s, and 1970s with the University of Utah taking the lead with many mound excavations across the state. Brigham Young University and the Antiquities Section in the Division of State History actively explored Fremont settlements, and universities from outside the state, including Harvard, University of California at Los Angeles (UCLA), University of Colorado, the Denver Museum of Natural History, as well as independent archaeological firms have also done research on Fremont sites. Their findings tell us much about this ancient society that flourished for over a thousand years.

The Fremont era began about 2,000 years ago and lasted until the mid-fourteenth century. The origin of the strategy known as the Fremont is still unresolved. Some argue that the farming way of life began as a result of a migration of people from the Southwest. Others have maintained that farming was gradually and unevenly adopted by residents whose primary means of subsistence came mostly by hunting and gathering wild foods. This hunter-gatherer lifestyle had endured for millennia in Utah and is usually referred to as the Archaic by archaeologists.

Archaeological findings to date suggest that farming, pottery making, pithouses,[1] and other Fremont farmer characteristics developed slowly. The key ingredient in the farming strategy, corn, appears north of the Colorado River by about 200 B.C. and apparently was carried northward along with the knowledge of how to farm and how to construct bell-shaped cists or pits to store the corn. These cists (which sometimes contain human burials) have been found at several places in the central and northeastern part of the state. In some places, shallow pithouses are adjacent to these cists. The Fremont were using bows and arrows by about A.D. 200 and making pottery by A.D. 500. Deep circular pithouses appear by A.D. 700 but shift to a rectangular shape by the A.D. 1100s. At some later sites, especially in the eastern Great Basin area, Fremont people built large, adobe-walled houses at ground level such as those seen at Nawthis Village east of Salina and at Baker Village on the Utah–Nevada border. By A.D. 1000 or earlier, storage had shifted from bell-shaped cists to small, one- and two-room surface granaries built next to residences and small adobe or masonry cists in remote, protected locations. A typical Fremont household often consisted of a pithouse with the storage structure close by. The presence of pithouses and granaries suggests the Fremont were settled or living permanently in one spot. However, the importance of hunting and gathering persisted even with those most committed to farming.

The best known of the Fremont lifeways is farming, which was practiced by those living in areas with good soils for raising corn, beans, and squash. These crops were originally domesticated much earlier in Mexico

---

[1]Pithouses are houses built by first excavating a pit, then constructing a roof over it. Pithouses are described in more detail in Chapter 2.

Rectangular pithouse, North Finger, Five Finger Ridge.

and eventually were obtained by peoples in Utah through borrowing or perhaps through the movement of people northward. The farmers are better known than other strategies simply because they crafted ceramics reminiscent of Anasazi pottery, built pithouses and granaries of adobe and stone, and sometimes congregated in villages. As a result, the places where these people lived are more visible and tend to be where modern cities or towns are located; consequently, more of these kinds of sites have been excavated and reported. Not all Fremont people were farmers, however. Some lived in more temporary brush houses and either did not farm or farmed only occasionally. For those reasons the sites where these people lived are less visible and only a few such sites have been explored by archaeologists. It should be noted, however, that farm products were available to all through exchange.

Some have argued that corn was more important to Fremont peoples on the Northern Colorado Plateau to the east than it was to those living along the eastern edge of the Great Basin. Reasons given for these differences are mostly environmental: desirable wild resources were more abundant along the Basin rim than on the Plateau and the need for corn was less. It is likely the case, however, that farming was never as important in the Fremont area as it was to the ancient Southwestern farmers such as the Anasazi and the Hohokam.[2] In fact, archaeologists working directly with human skeletal remains have now shown corn farming was not always practiced by those living near the Great Salt Lake and was abandoned in that area by A.D. 1150. Dietary studies tell us corn was a more significant part of the diet in central Utah. Hunting was always important, and the discarded bones of deer, mountain sheep, rabbits, fish, and birds litter Fremont garbage dumps. The emphasis on large game, when available, was typical. Wild plants seeds from grasses, sunflowers, pinyons, along with roots were at least as important as meat, but evidence of these foods is harder to find archaeologically.

The numbers of farming sites (and presumably Fremont populations) grew substantially between A.D. 800 and 1200. Growth was not constant but waxed and waned over the centuries and from region to region. The sites on the Northern Colorado Plateau tend to be smaller than those along the eastern Great Basin edge. Site locations vary as well. On the plateau many sites are on knolls or ridges, while in the Great Basin, sites are more commonly on alluvial fans, often under modern towns such as Provo, Payson, Nephi, Richfield, Parowan, and others. Five Finger Ridge and Radford Roost located on ridges in Clear Creek Canyon are obvious exceptions to the preference for stream mouths and may mark a late shift in settlement. Nonetheless, remains of villages or at least concentrations of pithouses documenting repeated use of favored areas are common on the lower reaches of streams in these Great Basin rim valleys.

Fremont architecture varied by geographical region and changed in shape over time. Residences were most often pithouses, either circular or rectangular. Structures at sites in central Utah were often made with adobe, especially the granaries, while those on the Colorado Plateau to the east often included stone in their construction. Typically, pithouses were made by excavating a large circular or rectangular pit (sometimes up to three feet deep) into the ground and, in some cases, lining it with either large boulders or adobe plaster. Good-sized roof beams laid in spiral fashion pointing inward toward a central smoke/entry hole were held up

---

[2]The Anasazi and Hohokam farmers were contemporary with the Fremont. The Anasazi cultures spread across southern Nevada, Utah, and Colorado and northern New Mexico and Arizona. Most archaeologists believe the modern Puebloan groups (Hopi, Zuni, Rio Grande Pueblos) are their descendants. The Hohokam were true desert people who lived farther south along the Gila and Salt Rivers where present day Phoenix and Tucson are now located.

Adobe-walled granary, Southwest Finger, Five Finger Ridge.

by large vertical posts located either around the edge of the house or directly in the floor. Clay-rimmed, circular fire hearths were constructed in the middle of the floor directly below the entry hole. The roof entry may have been carefully finished with adobe and beams in a manner similar to that seen at Coyote Granary investigated on the Clear Creek Project (see Chapter 2 page 29). Roofs were finished with alternating layers of smaller branches and twigs covered with adobe. Floors were sometimes packed with clay to stabilize pebbly or sandy sediments, but most were simply hard-packed earth. A ventilator tunnel entering the corner of the house brought fresh air in and swept the smoke up through the smoke hole.

The other common architectural form at late Fremont sites in the eastern Great Basin is the adobe-walled granary. At Five Finger Ridge these were one- or two-roomed structures typically measuring 5 feet by 9 feet in size. The height of the walls was probably not much more than three feet. These buildings did not contain the hearths and living debris (broken bones, pottery sherds, stone flakes) typical of pithouses. In some instances, small bins were constructed in the corners for storage of tools.

The Fremont period is marked by a distinctive art style that can be seen on rock art panels, on stone, bone and clay figurines, and painted pottery. The style includes trapezoidal human figures with elaborate headgear and hair styles, in rock art and figurines. Elegant handled pitchers, black-on-gray and black-on-white geometric patterns on bowls, and coffee-beanlike decorations applied around vessel necks are some of the classic Fremont ceramic forms and styles. Other craft items, basketry, moccasins, and bone gaming counters, are also distinctive. The unique Fremont moccasins, for example, were made from the skins of the lower legs of deer and mountain sheep in such a way that the dew claws or hocks were located on the sole.

Trade in exotic goods increased during the Fremont era. Marine shell (especially *Olivella*) from the Pacific Coast and turquoise probably mined in New Mexico, Arizona, or Nevada are the most common. Fremont artisans produced finely crafted jewelry from these exotics and from local minerals such as lignite, malachite, gypsum, selenite, and fluorite. Stones of green, blue, and red were clearly preferred for the manufacture of jewelry.

Bone was an important raw material for beads and pendants as well as bone dice or gaming counters. The abundance of often decorated, ochre-smeared and highly polished bone dice suggest the importance of gaming in Fremont society. These artifacts could also be indirect evidence of trading activities since gambling, feasting, and trading often went hand-in-hand in aboriginal North America.

Village Fremont society is usually described as simple with modest tendencies toward accumulation of wealth and status differentiation. However, the presence of significantly larger houses within villages and the tendency for labor-intensive, exotic goods to occur in the larger houses argues for some social climbing. Some individuals apparently achieved special status as evidenced by burials (adults males) found in Parowan Valley and in Huntington Canyon south of Price. Their status is suggested by the large quantity of grave goods: evidence for garments decorated with bird skins, grinding stones, figurines, and whole and/or broken

ceramic vessels. It is difficult for archaeologists to know what these artifacts are
telling us about the status of these men.
Perhaps they were shamans or individuals who had earned great respect during
their lives. They had clearly achieved
some special place since they were recognized in death with rare and relatively
abundant burial offerings.

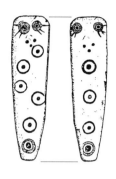

The Fremont farming strategy ended
by the middle of the fourteenth century
A.D. Farming, pithouses, thin-walled gray
ware and painted ceramics, trade in turquoise, and other material and organiza-
tional patterns disappeared. Archaeolo-

*Carved bone ornament from
Pithouse 57, Five Finger Ridge.*

gists have posed various explanations for the demise of the Fremont, but
most conclude a deterioration in the climate made corn farming too
risky. There seems to be some relationship between the changes that
occur in the Fremont area and those to the south as farming disappears in
the Four Corners area and regions north at roughly the same time. Some
have argued the change is related to migration, that a new group moving
east and north across the Great Basin pushed the Fremont out. Others
disagree, maintaining the Fremont did not move out; they only adjusted
their lifestyle to accommodate changes in the natural world. Most likely
the explanation is more complicated than either of these scenarios.

├────────────┤ **20 cm**

A rare pictoglyph from Site
42SV1928, Area B, Panel 105.

In restructuring work in the Fremont region, it seems most profitable to drop back to concentrated studies of communities, exploring in detail local systems of adaptation.

Patrick Hogan and Lynne Sebastian (1980)

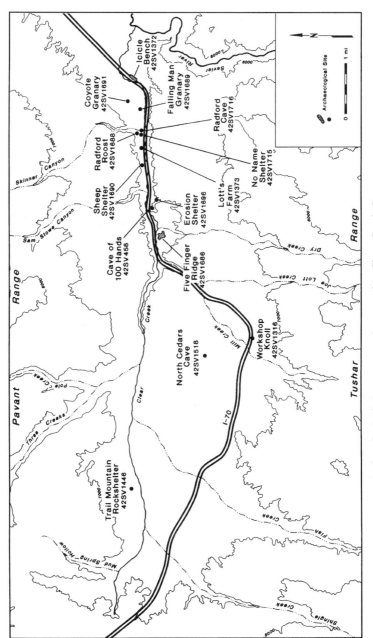

Archaeological sites excavated or tested in Clear Creek Canyon.

2

The Clear Creek Canyon Archaeological Project

The Introduction offered a brief history of the Clear Creek Canyon Archaeological Project including the number of participants, but some expansion of that history seems appropriate. The Office of Public Archaeology at Brigham Young University, for example, did not become involved in the project until the fall of 1983 with the work at Icicle Bench. It was at this time that Bob Leonard, archaeologist for the Fishlake National Forest, organized tours of the excavations to educate local school children about archaeology and the importance of preserving sites. Steven Magleby, a student at Monroe Elementary, was one of those who toured Icicle Bench. He later returned to the canyon to see the excavations with his father; however, Mr. Magleby drove past Icicle Bench and instead visited a site he had known about for a number of years. They were surprised to find bulldozers were preparing to use the hill the site was on for highway fill. Concerned, Mr. Magleby contacted state agencies and the archaeologists working at Icicle Bench. Shortly afterwards, archaeologists visited and recorded the site and, based on the presence of house depressions and abundant surface artifacts, concluded this was a large Fremont village that needed protection.

The discovery of Five Finger Ridge lead to dramatic expansion in the size of the research project. To obtain a more complete perspective on how past peoples had used the canyon, archaeologists decided to look for sites in a number of areas in the canyon uplands as well as the creek bottom. Not only were large pithouse sites excavated, but several smaller sites, including some caves or rockshelters, were tested. It was hoped that looking at different kinds of sites in different settings would provide a more complete picture of Fremont use of the canyon. Such a regional perspective had not been attempted in the past. As part of this broader approach, an effort was made to locate and record the many rock art panels in the canyon. The Paiute Tribe of Utah played an important role in the rock art study and several tribal members served on crews and directed excavations during the project. The work began in November of 1983 at Icicle Bench and continued there until January of 1984, when research began at Radford Roost. Crews started excavations at Five Finger Ridge shortly after and continued until the fall of 1984. The surveys and small site testing were also completed during 1984. Rock art work lingered until the late 1980s.

The project was challenging in a number of respects. The scheduling of the excavations during the winter made work for the crews miserable. Work at Icicle Bench and Radford Roost was slowed because the ground was often wet or frozen, making screening difficult. Waiting for better weather was impossible given the deadlines for highway construction. At Five Finger Ridge, bulldozers were removing portions of the site as soon as the archaeologists were through. Nonetheless, the project was exciting, especially the work at Five Finger Ridge. It seemed the entire hill was a solid mass of houses and other evidences of living. The crews were in a state of head-shaking disbelief at the never-ending discoveries. To find houses or activity areas, crews dug narrow, shallow trenches across the hillside. An abrupt change in soil color and texture, from light tan to the dark, charcoal specks of ancient midden, signaled another house or a work area outside the house. The archaeologists would then trench across the darkly stained soil to find the other side of the house, dig a test pit along the edge to find the floor, and then remove the dirt inside the structure.

As noted in the Introduction, all the artifacts and other information recovered during the Clear Creek research have been described in a multivolume technical report submitted to the Utah Department of Transportation and all artifacts are stored at the Fremont Indian State Park.

The Surveys
Surface and Rock Art Surveys

Archaeological survey systematically examines the ground surface for evidence of past human activity such as pottery sherds, flakes of stone produced during tool making, evidence of buried houses, charcoal stains, glass, old nails, and other such things. Survey work related to highway construction included several ground surveys, a rock art survey by archaeologists, and a rock art survey carried out and written up under the direction of the Paiute Tribe of Utah (see Martineau 1985 in Additional Readings).

Ground Surveys

Ground surveys in Clear Creek Canyon began in 1976 when archaeologists walked the highway right-of-way, or the ground that would actually be disturbed during the construction of I-70. This survey covered the area from Clear Creek Summit east through the canyon to the town of Joseph. This survey work identified Workshop Knoll, Lott's Farm, and Icicle Bench as well as smaller archaeological sites. Other surveys located Radford Roost, Radford Cave, Sheep Shelter, and No Name Shelter as well as numerous rock art sites. Leads from local residents provided more information about archaeological sites in the canyon and federal (Forest Service and Bureau of Land Management) archaeologists documented three more sheltered sites, Trail Mountain Shelter, Erosion Shelter, and North Cedars Cave, along with two granaries, Coyote and Falling Man. Finally, archaeologists looked at 60 blocks of land varying in size from 7 to 40 acres each in the uplands above the canyon bottom. During these surveys, 94 archaeological sites (excluding rock art sites) were recorded. These varied in age from about 10,000 years ago up to the historic era, in elevation from about 5,500 feet up to over 8,000 feet, and in size from a few square feet to many thousands of square feet.

Dating of the surveyed sites relied on the presence of time sensitive artifacts, usually arrow or atlatl points, found on the surface. Since most stone projectile point types have been dated by radiocarbon in buried sites, stone arrow and atlatl points[1] enable archaeologists to sort sites or site components by time period (many sites showed evidence of use by peoples during very different time periods). One was considered Paleoindian in age, 15 were Archaic, 28 were Fremont, 8 were Late Prehistoric, and 7 were historic. The remainder could not be sorted by time. Of the 94 sites found, 13 were partially or wholly excavated. These periods and their presumed ages are described in more detail in Chapter 3.

---

[1] The term projectile point is used by archaeologists to include both atlatl and arrow points. The former are typically much larger than the latter as they were used to tip long (3–4 feet) darts propelled by a throwing stick or atlatl. Arrow points were, of course, used to tip the shorter arrows for use with bows. Atlatls were the primary hunting tool in Utah until about A.D. 200 when the bow became widespread.

Archaeologist recording one of the hundreds of rock art panels in Clear Creek Canyon.

Rock Art Surveys

Clear Creek Canyon rock art was well known before this project. Descriptions of the panels were made by Neil Judd, an archaeologist who did research in Utah in the 1910s and 1920s (see Judd's 1926 publication in Additional Readings), and well-known historian Frank Beckwith who mentions them in his book *Millard and Nearby.* Rock art, both painted (pictographs) and pecked (petroglyphs), as well as historic (more than fifty years old) signatures, are abundant in the canyon. Project participants recognized the importance of documenting this highly visible expression of early peoples. As noted, two different kinds of surveys were focused on the rock art: (1) a traditional survey with the primary purpose of documenting as completely and accurately as possible, and (2) an interpretive survey carried out with a Native American perspective. The sheer quantity of rock art, thousands of elements and hundreds of panels spread over 43 archaeological sites, made this an extremely time consuming and difficult task. The panels were photographed multiple times and, in some cases, videotaped, drawn, and described. The rock art is described in more detail in Chapter 5.

The Excavations

Sheltered Sites

Seven rockshelter or cave sites were partially excavated. Three of the sheltered sites, Radford Cave, No Name Shelter and Erosion Shelter contained very little evidence of human occupation and are not discussed. Sheep Shelter, North Cedars Cave, Trail Mountain Shelter, and to a certain extent Cave of 100 Hands, were more heavily used by Archaic, Fremont, and perhaps the ancestors of Southern Paiute or Ute peoples. Site locations are plotted on the map on page 18.

20 cm

*Fremont-style rock art with abstracted human figures,
mountain sheep, and perhaps deer.*

Cave of 100 Hands–the rows of reddish orange handprints are barely visible on the back wall of the cave.

Cave of 100 Hands

Cave of 100 Hands (42SV458)[2] gets its name from the numerous reddish orange handprints pressed on the rock wall at the back of the cave. This site was well known and had been visited many times in the past. For example, in May of 1937, Elmer Smith of the University of Utah visited this cave and excavated a small test pit near the back wall. Later the same year John Gillin, representing both the University of Utah and the Peabody Museum at Harvard University, revisited and excavated more of the site. Neither encountered much in the way of artifacts. Excavations here during the Clear Creek research verified that the site was little used in the past, although a hearth dating to the Fremont period was found. The cave's north-facing location on the south side of the

---

[2]This numeric and alphabetic code is a means of designating archaeological sites that is widely used in the United States. The system was devised by the Smithsonian Institution and is, therefore, called the Smithsonian Trinomial System. The number 42 stands for the state of Utah (Utah is number 42 in an alphabetized list of the states), SV stands for Sevier County, and 458 simply means that 457 sites were recorded in Sevier County before Cave of 100 Hands. Since sites are sometimes given different names by different peoples, the Smithsonian Trinomial System is used to avoid confusion much like Latin is used internationally to refer to plant and animal taxa. All sites recorded on the project were given similar, although unique, numbers.

*These mountain sheep were pecked into the rock just inside
the opening to Sheep Shelter.*

creek may explain why it was not often occupied. North-facing caves are much less likely to contain evidence of human occupation, presumably because they receive less in the way of solar heat. However, important information about past climates was obtained from Cave of 100 Hands using pollen collected from the cave sediments.

Sheep Shelter

Sheep Shelter (42SV1690) was also named for associated rock art. Pecked panels of bighorn sheep were found inside and above the shelter entrance as well as on the cliff face just outside the entrance. This small shelter is on the north side of the creek at the base of the cliff face. As with Cave of 100 Hands, use of Sheep Shelter was rather light; however, several hearths (remains of ancient camp fires) were found at varying levels in the six or more feet of deposits with the deepest dating to nearly 3,500 B.C. In fact, Sheep Shelter was occupied mostly during the Archaic rather than the Fremont period and is the best evidence obtained during the project pertaining to this earlier time. Artifacts were scarce in the site, but, as with the other sheltered sites, the pollen data obtained has contributed to the reconstruction of past environments (see **How Do Scientists Reconstruct Past Climates?** in Chapter 4 on page 64).

North Cedars Cave

North Cedars Cave (42SV1518) is a small lava tube in the uplands above and to the south of Clear Creek that was often used during the Fremont and post–Fremont eras. The site had been discovered by collectors prior to the project and had been badly disturbed by amateur digging. This disturbance greatly reduced the quality of the recoverable information, since the rich deposits were churned making comparisons through time nearly impossible. Still, the presence of Fremont and Late Prehistoric ceramics and radiocarbon dates ranging from A.D. 1000 to A.D. 1700 are evidence of long-term, sporadic occupation.

Trail Mountain Rockshelter

Trail Mountain Shelter is located under a slight overhang at the base of a large outcrop of volcanic rock on the north side of Clear Creek in the upper part of the canyon. The area where people stayed in the past is only marginally protected from the elements but, nevertheless, had been used as a camping area by both Fremont and Late Prehistoric peoples. As with North Cedars Cave, considerable digging for artifacts had occurred here, again reducing the value of the recovered data. Radiocarbon dates and ceramics place the primary use of the site in the Fremont period, with some later occupation.

Storage Sites or Granaries

Two of the most interesting sites explored during the project were storage areas, Coyote Granary and Falling Man Granary, located well away from the large village sites along the creek. Although most archaeologists agree that granaries such as these likely were constructed by peoples living in the pithouse villages, it is not known which peoples (from Radford Roost? Icicle Bench? Five Finger Ridge?) built them and how they might have been used. Who, for example, stored things here? Was it a communal storage area for seed corn? How were these storage facilities different from the storage granaries alongside the pithouses at Radford Roost and Five Finger Ridge? These questions remain largely unanswered, but the presence of these facilities are evidence of long-term planning by Fremont farmers.

Coyote Granary nestled against the rock overhang.
The adobe, lipped opening is clearly visible.

Coyote Granary

Coyote Granary (42SV1691) sits in a small canyon north of Clear Creek Canyon not far from Icicle Bench. The granary was made of adobe and wooden beams. It is a small, finely crafted structure, about 6 feet by 3 feet on the inside, and that area is subdivided. The entrance was through a small, lipped opening in the top of the granary. The roof was elaborately made from several mats of woven twigs all of which had been sealed with a layer of adobe. Artifacts were scarce, but pieces of corn cobs and pine nut shells as well as juniper seeds and bark were all present in the fill. Some of those things might have been brought in by pack rats, but the corn and the pine nuts must have been carried here by humans, since neither are available in the vicinity. Radiocarbon dates from roofing material place the construction of the granary either in the A.D. 700s or the A.D. 1000s.

A close-up of roof construction from inside Coyote Granary.

Falling Man Granary

Falling Man granary (42SV1689) lies in the lower reaches of Clear Creek Canyon high on the north side along a narrow ledge. A rock art panel with classic Fremont anthropomorphs (figures shaped like people) confronts visitors to the site. The granary is built into a natural alcove in the cliff face. Larger than Coyote Granary, (13 feet by 3 feet interior dimensions), Falling Man was also built using adobe and some small beams, although adobe was used more sparingly here and stone slabs were more important. Like Coyote, the most interesting finds were plant remains. Corn, cactus, juniper, pinyon, and oak were all represented in the excavated fill. Corn is the only nonlocal item, however, and must have been brought to the site by people. What is curious is that many of the cob fragments were charred. Unless the granary and its contents had been burned (there is no evidence of this), the presence of charred cobs is puzzling. A single arrow point was found on the surface just outside the granary. The two radiocarbon dates from structural wood are similar to those from Coyote Granary and are also widely separated in time, ca. A.D. 685 and A.D. 1000 (estimated ages).

Rock art panel near Falling Man Granary. The granary is nestled under an overhang to the left of the boulder not containing rock art.

Residential or Structural Sites

Three structural (containing the remains of houses) sites were excavated by Brigham Young University during the Clear Creek Project: Icicle Bench at the mouth of the canyon, Radford Roost a mile or so up from the canyon mouth, and Five Finger Ridge near the juncture of Mill and Clear Creeks. An additional structural site, Lott's Farm, was excavated in 1981 by the Antiquities Section at the Utah Division of State History. Lott's Farm was on the Clear Creek floodplain about a quarter mile west, or upstream, from Radford Roost.

Icicle Bench

Icicle Bench (42SV1372) lay in an alfalfa field on the Clear Creek floodplain at the mouth of Clear Creek Canyon. It was named by the crews who excavated here in the winter of 1983–1984 in recognition of the frigid working conditions. Much of the initial exploration of the site was done by backhoe trenching. During that work five pithouses, four outside work areas, and a burial, were found. In addition, 13 less obvious features[3] were exposed in the backhoe trenches; some of these were clearly hearths or pits, but the function of others could not be identified. These features were, in some cases, sampled to recover charcoal for dates but were not explored further. Icicle Bench was totally destroyed during highway construction.

Perhaps the most interesting aspect of this site is that it was used many times over a very long period. Radiocarbon dates from excavated features range from about 500 B.C. to the 1200s A.D. The earliest date (about 450 B.C.) was obtained from Activity Area 1, while the latest came from Pit Structure 5 (A.D. 1290). The earliest house excavated at Icicle Bench and on the Clear Creek Project was Pit Structure 2, which dated to about A.D. 425. Excavation crews began to speculate about the early age of this house when it became clear that there was no pottery in association with the floor. This large house (20 feet in diameter) was circular and had burned, leaving the roof beams in place, clearly showing the pattern of construction with timbers radiating inward like spokes on a wheel. The much smaller Pit Structure 1 was constructed later into the fill of Pit Structure 2. The excavations of the pithouses at Icicle Bench reveal the evolution of residential architectural form from circular prior to A.D. 900 to more rectangular after that period.

Icicle Bench was also notable for the absence of adobe-walled storage houses or granaries. As mentioned earlier, these structures are a common part of Fremont household facilities, especially after about A.D. 1000. The fact that none of these structures were found at Icicle Bench could be due to the disturbance of the ground surface by farming. But it could also be bad luck; that is, the backhoe testing did not happen to encounter any granaries. Also scarce here were artifacts in general. Bone, ceramics, and chipped stone tools and debitage (debris generated when making chipped stone tools like arrow heads) were not abundant at this site. The single exception to this pattern was Activity Area 4 where stone flakes and other material remains were more numerous. This area may have been a kind of garbage dump or midden during an early period of occupation (Activity Area 4 dates to A.D. 900s) as no hearths or other features were found here.

---

[3]Features are terms archaeologists use to refer to just about anything they may see during excavation that requires further investigation. Most features are eventually fully excavated, and, once their function, shapes, etc., are known, given some understandable label like house or hearth or stratum.

Excavating the granary at Radford Roost, early winter of 1984.

Radford Roost

Aptly named for its perchlike position on the north side of Clear Creek, Radford Roost[4] (42SV1688) sat on a prominent ridge about 50 feet above the creek bottom a mile up the canyon from Icicle Bench. Site architecture consisted of a deeply buried, roughly rectangular pithouse and a two-roomed, adobe-walled granary lying just upslope from the house. The promontory containing Radford Roost was completely removed to make room for the highway.

The pithouse at Radford Roost was large, about 17 feet on a side, and deep, the floor being close to 3 feet below ground surface. The walls were carefully plastered with thick (6–12 inches) adobe to hold the gravelly sediments in place. A clay-rimmed hearth was in the center of the rather poorly preserved floor. The house also contained some puzzling features, most notably a low (2–12 inches high) ridge constructed of adobe that ran roughly parallel to and a short distance from the walls. The ridge may have been part of a bench or perhaps was a partition related to the ventilation system in the house. The ridge may have kept cold air coming in from the ventilator shaft (see the narrow trench at the

---

[4]Named after the Radford family who owned the property.

Pithouse at Radford Roost fully excavated.

upper left hand part of the house in the accompanying photo) from spreading across the floor where the occupants would have been sitting. The dirt fill of the house was homogenous with no evidence of layering. This fact suggests that, for some reason, the house was purposefully filled in after the roof beams had been removed. Artifacts were abundant in the fill and on the floor of the pit structure. Numerous arrow points, bone tools, pottery fragments, several *Olivella* shell (seashells from the Pacific Coast) beads, and other artifacts came from this single structure. The reasons for the density of artifacts is not clear, but the area had been heavily used.

The two-roomed granary lay up the ridge slope about 20 feet north of the house. The rooms were about 7 feet square and enclosed by walls up to 14 inches thick and 16 inches high, although they were probably much higher when in use. The floors of both rooms had been carefully prepared of adobe and had been laid as a single floor over the entire structure with the partition added at a later time. Wild tobacco seeds found on the floor of the granary may be evidence of the use of this plant either for smoking or medicinal purposes.

Dating Radford Roost proved to be difficult as radiocarbon samples ranged in age from about A.D. 300 to the late A.D. 1100s. In all probability

What Was It Like to Live in a Pithouse?

Imagine a late December day in A.D. *1280. A cold wind sweeps down Clear Creek Canyon protesting your ascent up the Five Finger Ridge Trail. On the high knoll above, adobe granaries and roofed-over patios are visible under a thin blanket of snow. Smokey wisps from the several pithouses just below the ridge tells you someone is home. At the top, finally, you hurry to your destination and descend the notched log ladder engulfed by the smoke and warmth from the small central fire below, its clay rim protecting the floor mats from sparks. Inside it is warm and close, rich with the smells and sounds of living. The single, squarish room is roughly 12 feet on a side. You stoop to miss the beams holding up a thick roof, cross-hatched with small branches, cornstalks, and grasses sealed by a heavy layer of dirt. Post supports around the edge of the house hold the roof in place. The house is etched into the slope of the hill and the uphill walls are patched over with adobe. The dirt floor, thinly spread with sand, is mostly covered with soft juniper bark mats, especially toward the back where mats are piled for sleeping. Cache pits dug into the floor and lined with the same matting, hold food or tools. Other gear is tucked into crannies and hangs from the roof beams.*

The woman acknowledges your arrival and returns to grinding last fall's pine nuts on the metate next to the hearth. The man abandons reworking an obsidian tool and greets you from his seat against the uphill wall, offering a stubby clay pipe. You collapse on the mats and, smiling, help yourself to the meaty stew in a ceramic pot next to the fire. Two young children giggle in a corner playing with wooden toys under the watchful eye of the grandmother mending deerskin clothing. She uses several different bone needles and awls from a basketful of similar tools to sew the patches. Winter is the time for storytelling, and she sings softly to herself as she thinks about the next story of coyote and his never-ending pranks she will tell to her grandchildren.

This somewhat fanciful story is based (mostly) on the excavations of the many pithouses at Five Finger Ridge. These houses were efficient. The surrounding dirt insulated the inhabitants from winter cold and summer heat. During the warm months people probably spent little time inside the houses except to sleep. Interiors would have been fairly dark and smoky at all times of the year with the only light coming through the central opening and from the constant fire. Pithouses were the most common type of living quarters used during the Fremont period, although some lived in abode-walled houses built at ground surface. More information on Fremont architecture is contained in Chapters 1 and 4.

Pithouse 3, a typical rectangular house at Five Finger Ridge.

Drawing of what a typical pithouse may have looked like at Five Finger Ridge.

these discrepancies are a function of dating charcoal from wood that was older than the occupation of the house (see **How Long was Five Finger Ridge Occupied?** found in this chapter on page 42). When other time-sensitive artifacts such as ceramics and arrow points are considered, the later date seems to be the most likely age for the occupation of the site. Radford Roost was probably built in the twelfth or thirteenth century A.D. and used intensively before abandonment. The prominent location of the pithouse and the abundance of material remains may be evidence that those who lived here were important in the canyon community.

Lott's Farm

Lott's Farm (42SV1373) was located on the Clear Creek floodplain about 1,600 feet west of Radford Roost. The site is named after the historic owner of the property, Joe Lott, who settled in the canyon in the 1870s. This was the only historic, Euro-American site excavated as a consequence of highway construction in the canyon. The excavations were done by the Antiquities Section of the Utah Division of State History. The historic architecture investigated included a log cabin, stable, corral, and storage cellar. (To read more about the history of Lott's Farm and the descriptions of the excavation findings see Hawkins and Dobra 1982 in Additional Readings.) During the excavation and research of the historic farm, Fremont buildings were discovered. The front porch of the cabin was built over the Fremont granary, while the back porch lay over a portion of a pithouse. Also present were Late Prehistoric artifacts: several Paiute-style pottery sherds, a scraping tool of purple glass, and stone and metal arrow points.

The style of Fremont architecture at Lott's Farm fits comfortably into the late period of the Fremont occupation in the canyon. A deep (nearly 5 feet) square pithouse measuring about 13 feet on a side was found along with a two-roomed, abode-walled granary about 20 feet to the north. In the space between the pithouse and the granary, was a small (about 6 feet diameter), somewhat unusual, circular cist or storage feature with what appeared to be postholes around the outer edge of the bottom or floor. It is possible that this feature is similar to the secondary pit structures found at Five Finger Ridge up the canyon (see below).

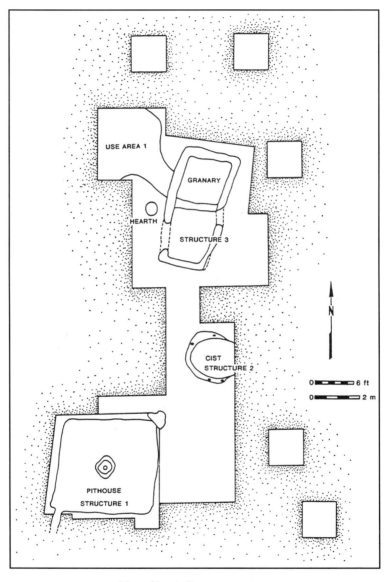

Map of Lott's Farm excavations.

Overview of the east ridge at Five Finger Ridge during excavations.

The radiocarbon dates from the site suggest a late Fremont occupation for the house, around A.D. 1290. The array of artifacts and dates recovered during the excavation of the Lott's Farm site demonstrates the location had been attractive to people for at least two thousand years. That use varied from short-term stays during the Archaic and Late Prehistoric to more permanent residences during the Fremont and Historic periods. The Fremont constructions at Lott's Farm were not visible without excavation, which makes one wonder whether additional Fremont houses are buried along the creek.

Interestingly, the prehistoric use of Lott's Farm was not limited to the Fremont era but spans the period from the late Archaic to the Late Prehistoric. One of the several backhoe trenches placed around the cabin revealed a hearth deeper than the other exposed features and dated to about 150 B.C.

Five Finger Ridge

Five Finger Ridge (42SV1686) is the largest concentration of Fremont period houses and associated architectural features excavated to date. The background on its discovery was presented earlier, but it is worth repeating that the site was not found during the several archaeological surveys related to I-70 construction. Members of the concerned and interested public alerted archaeologists to the presence of the site. It escaped discovery because it was not in the direct path (right-of-way) of the highway or power lines; consequently, no investigation had been directed to this location. Instead, the sage- and grass-covered hill where the site was located was destined for complete removal for highway fill and bulldozers had already cut trails up the slopes and across the central saddle area when the archaeologists arrived.

The series of ridges upon which the site lay inspired archaeologists to label the locale Five Finger Ridge. The site lay on the south side of Clear Creek about a half mile down the canyon from the confluence of Mill and Clear Creeks. Fremont Indian State Park is now located almost directly across (north) the creek from where the site was. Explaining why the Fremont chose this hilltop location to build has inspired much discussion. Ideas range from offering a better vantage up and down the canyon to staying free of bugs (more wind up on the hill), to staying warm (more sunshine up high). Such explanations are elusive and the real reasons will always be a matter of conjecture. We do know that, for whatever reason, the Fremont populations of Clear Creek Canyon concentrated here during the twelfth, thirteenth, and fourteenth centuries A.D. They constructed well over 100 architectural features, 37 of which were pithouses, 19 were abode-walled surface granaries, and 23 were small or secondary pit structures that appeared to serve some special use other than living quarters. Unique architecture at the site included a square house built on the surface with rather thin adobe walls and a jacal[5] structure. This jacal (pronounced "ha call" with the accent on the last syllable) house (?) apparently did not have a south wall, although a substantial roof was likely present given the size of the main support postholes. Interestingly, this jacal structure, the square surface house, and the largest pithouse on the site were all clustered in the center of the site where all the ridges come together. Was this a coincidence? Some ideas as to what this might mean are presented in Chapter 4 on page 71 under "Village Planning and Household Structures."

---

[5]Jacal consists of small poles set upright to form walls that are then covered or supported with adobe. This kind of construction, which is also referred to as wattle-and-daub, is different from the walls of granaries that were constructed with large adobe blocks laid in courses similar to bricks.

Jacal house(?) near the top of the ridge after excavation.
The pattern of upright posts is clearly visible around the walls.

Drawing of how the jacal house may have looked when it was in use.
The building behind it is a pithouse.

How Long Was Five Finger Ridge Occupied?

Five Finger Ridge has more dates from radiocarbon assay, archaeomagnetism, dendrochronology, and obsidian hydration than any other archaeological site in Utah. Sixty-one radiocarbon dates from 43 structures and 1 activity area, 41 archaeomagnetic determinations from 31 structures and associated areas, 9 tree-ring ages from 4 structures, and 14 obsidian hydration dates from 5 structures were obtained from the site. In addition, ceramic and stratigraphic information were used to assist in relative age estimates.

The heavy emphasis on dating at Five Finger Ridge was related to the project's research interest in Fremont social life and community organization. If the archaeologists are to make a good argument that houses and granaries were laid out according to some plan, they must first determine whether those constructions all date to the same time. Most fundamental in determining whether houses were contemporary are stratigraphic relationships. If houses are built on top of one another (or superimposed), it is clear that they cannot be the same age. Sites occupied over and over again tend to contain superimposed houses, usually in a preferred location. Of course, simply because houses are not built on top of each other doesn't mean they are contemporary.

As we attempted to understand the site and what appeared to be some evidence of planning, we posed the issue of contemporaneity as a problem that dating techniques could help us solve. As noted, stratigraphy was the most basic of concerns in resolving this issue. It was clear during excavations that there were few instances of overlapping houses or other constructions, even along the ridge or just below the ridge crest, where most houses where found. Sensing the stratigraphic data could be suggesting that many of the houses were occupied at once, we turned to the several absolute dating techniques mentioned above.

Radiocarbon dating was by far the most useful dating tool employed at the site. A concern with radiocarbon dates is that people tend to gather dead wood for cooking fires and to re-use beams for house building. Charcoal from beams as well as charcoal from hearths, therefore, have a high probability of dating older than the true date of use. To allow for this problem, ages for the houses were routinely assigned based on the most recent dates. Relying on careful and conservative evaluations of the radiocarbon dates and other data noted above, archaeologists concluded that Five Finger Ridge was occupied mostly between A.D. 1200 and 1300 (see accompanying graph).

The data on this graph, then, is the payoff for the investment made by the archaeologists in multiple dating techniques. First, the dates tell us the primary use of the site was quite late in the Fremont sequence. Second, and more pertinent to the research interests, these dates along with supporting stratigraphic data strengthen the argument for many of the houses being occupied at the same time.

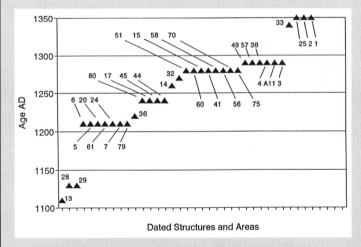

Radiocarbon dates from houses at Five Finger Ridge (the numbers represent individual houses or granaries).

How Do These Dating Techniques Work?

Radiocarbon dating, certainly the most commonly used dating tool in the United States, is based on the assumption that all living matter contains a known percentage of carbon 14, an unstable and heavy isotope of carbon (normal atomic weight of carbon is 12) that decays at a constant rate (one half of the carbon 14 decays every 5,730 years). Once an organism dies, the carbon 14 continues to decay, and the amount left can be measured allowing scientists to estimate the age of the sample being analyzed. The advantage of radiocarbon dating is that remains of once-living things (charcoal, wood, bark, bone) are quite common in archaeological sites.

Tree-ring dating (dendrochronology) is based on the assumption that trees grow annual rings and the width of the rings varies with climatic conditions. The patterns of wide and narrow rings are unique and can be matched with patterns of known age. Tree-ring dating is very accurate (to the year in some cases), but samples are only occasionally available. Certain trees (pine, for example) are more useful for tree-ring dating as they always produce annual growth rings; others (such as juniper) are not so reliable.

Archaeomagnetism is based on the knowledge that the magnetic north pole has migrated over the centuries and its position has been established for various times in the past. Sediments, such as clays that are used in house construction or to line hearths, often contain particles of iron. Under certain conditions, especially when a house or hearth is burned, those clay particles align with the location of the earth's magnetic field at that time. By taking samples of the clay (it has to be part of an unmoved feature) and carefully marking the direction of today's magnetic north, the magnetic orientation of the sample can be determined and the age of the last firing estimated.

Obsidian hydration dating is based on the fact that freshly broken obsidian (volcanic glass) absorbs water, building a sort of skin or rind on the artifact, and that rind can be measured and age estimates made.

Stone pipe (a), bone tools (b), and arrow point (c) in place after a large, corrugated jar was removed from a Five Finger Ridge pithouse. These items were apparently stored in the jar.

The remainder of the features at the site were mostly outside work areas. The presence of hearths and occasional postholes here suggest that the work space was covered with a sunshade or ramada. Borrow pits (places from which the Fremont took dirt) and several more constructions of unknown function also were found.

Dating the many houses at Five Finger Ridge was an important goal. Determining which houses were being used at the same time would allow archaeologists to make more accurate estimates of how many people had lived here in the past. Dating tools used were radiocarbon, tree ring, obsidian hydration, and archaeomagnetism (see **"How Do These Dating**

Techniques Work? on page 44). The most useful of these techniques turned out to be radiocarbon dating and over 60 samples of charcoal were submitted. Based on the radiocarbon data, Five Finger Ridge was a late Fremont site occupied primarily between A.D. 1200 and 1300. A few dates suggest some use in the early A.D. 1100s and some people lingered until A.D. 1350 or so. Given that specific absolute calendrical dates (A.D. 1492, for example), cannot be achieved with any of the tools available to archaeologists on such sites, it could be that these estimates are somewhat in error. Chances are good, however, that they are an accurate reflection of the true age of the site.

The quantity of artifacts found during the excavation of Five Finger Ridge is high, numbering in the many thousands. Most, of course, are bits of stone, pottery, and bone with only a small percentage of complete items. Nonetheless, whole artifacts (chipped stone tools such as arrow points and knives, grinding stones, and bone tools, especially awls) were common. Complete ceramic vessels and decorative items, on the other hand, were rare. Unlike Anasazi sites where whole vessels are fairly common, complete pots are seldom found in the Fremont area. The discovery of six whole vessels in one of the pithouses was, therefore, quite surprising. Other unusual finds included fragments of basketry, hide, and wooden objects that were preserved due to the fact that they were protected from moisture by either being inside ceramic vessels or because they were so deeply buried. Also unusual was the number of turquoise pendants and beads recovered (53). In part, these finds are a function of the scale of the excavations (the more you dig, the more you find).

In addition to these material objects recovered from Five Finger Ridge, the archaeologists who studied the site were also interested in recovering nonmaterial information about the structure of the society, trading activities, and population levels. These and other topics are discussed in Chapter 4.

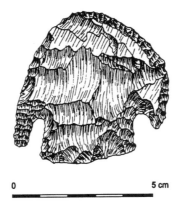

0   5 cm

Hafted scraper found in Sheep Shelter.

From 10,000 or more years ago, until A.D. 400, the only culture represented in Utah as well as the rest of the Great Basin was the Desert Archaic. That culture is characterized as a hunting-gathering one, a flexible, highly adaptable lifeway that has characterized most of man's worldwide history.

From A.D. 400 to A.D. 1200 to 1300 there is a change. Most of Utah was occupied by Fremont peoples with a horticultural subsistence. . . . Here reference is to the practice of cultivation of corn, squash, and beans, and the making of pottery.

Jesse D. Jennings (1978)

Clear Creek Canyon Chronology

	Description	Pottery Sequence	Projectile Point Sequence
A.D. 1860	**HISTORIC** Lott's Farm and other European settlements.		
A.D. 1400	**LATE PREHISTORIC** Use of Trail Mountain Shelter and North Cedars Cave.		
A.D. 1200	**FREMONT** Heaviest occupation at Five Finger Ridge, Radford Roost, Lott's Farm. Late houses at Icicle Bench occupied.		
A.D. 100–500	Last use of Sheep Shelter. Early Fremont/Late Archaic occupation at Icicle Bench.		
3500 B.C.	**ARCHAIC** Heaviest use of Sheep Shelter. Earliest use of Sheep Shelter and earliest date in Clear Creek Canyon.		
8000 B.C.	**PALEOINDIAN** Possible Paleoindian presence.		

Aerial view of Five Finger Ridge during excavation, spring 1984.

The east finger of Five Finger Ridge during excavation.
Clear Creek is visible in the background.

Excavating a pithouse on Five Finger Ridge.

Rock art with textile design in Clear Creek Canyon.

Arrow points from Five Finger Ridge.

Large corrugated ceramic vessel from a pithouse in Five Finger Ridge.

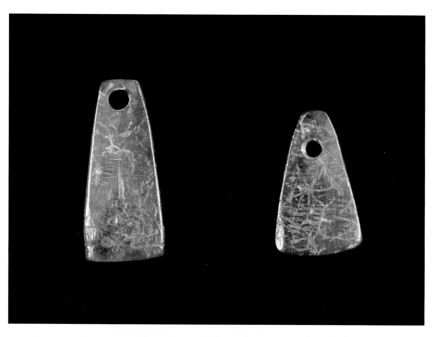

Bone pendants from Five Finger Ridge. (Largest pendant is 3 cm long.)

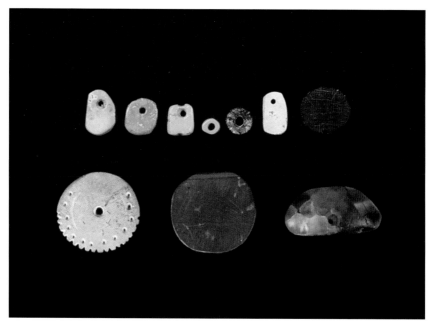

Pendants and bead of turquoise, lignite, siltstone, and fluorite.
(Not to same scale. Pendants on top row are about 1 cm in width;
those on the bottom are about 3.5 cm in diameter.)

3

History of Clear Creek Canyon

Early Canyon Peoples

How long ago did people begin living in Clear Creek Canyon? It is possible that exploration and use began with the Paleoindian period (6500 to 10,000 B.C.). A fragment of a fluted projectile point[1] (probably used on a throwing spear or atlatl) was found in the canyon in 1989 (see Larsen 1990 in Additional Readings). This artifact could not be directly dated, but similar projectile points from the Great Plains are known to be of Paleoindian age. The artifact was made of obsidian from the Mineral Mountain area to the west (see **Where Did People Obtain Obsidian?** in Chapter 4 on page 82). This surface find suggests that people were using Mineral Mountain obsidian 10,000 years ago, even though it is very possible that the point fragment was dropped in the canyon much later. An obsidian Clovis point from Texas was also traced to the Mineral Mountains and is further evidence that local obsidian was known and used during the Paleoindian period. Beyond knowing that they were here, we can say little about what people did so many years ago in central Utah. In other parts of North America, especially on the Great Plains to the east of the Rocky Mountains, Paleoindian peoples actively hunted mammoth and long-horned bison with projectile points similar to those made of Mineral Mountain obsidian. But no archaeological sites have been found in Utah or the Great Basin, for that matter, that contain clear evidence of people hunting these now-extinct mammals. It is doubtful the heroic hunter lifeway existed in the Great Basin given the current evidence. A

---

[1]Fluted projectile points are considered to be Paleoindian in age. The two known, fluted-point styles characteristic of this era are called Clovis and Folsom, and they are dated to about 11,000 and 1,000 years ago respectively.

more reasonable assumption is that an Archaic lifestyle (see below) was in place at this early date.[2]

The earliest evidence of people in the canyon recovered during the Clear Creek Project came from Sheep Shelter and represents what has come to be called the Archaic period in Utah's pre-European history. The Archaic is a several-thousand-year era during which people depended on wild plants and animals for food. Dietary emphasis varied depending on locally available resources. Most of the evidence for this period comes from large caves that were heavily used for living and storing tools and foodstuffs. It is perhaps predictable, therefore, that the earliest dates on the project came from a cavelike site. Hearths in the bottom layers of this small rock shelter dated to nearly 3,500 B.C., or the middle of the Archaic period. In fact, the heaviest use of Sheep Shelter was by Archaic peoples, but it must be remembered the Archaic period, as documented at Sheep Shelter, lasted at least from 3,500 B.C. to A.D. 500, a span of 4,000 years. The Fremont period lasted from A.D. 500 to A.D. 1350 or so, a span of only 800 years. Certainly we would expect more evidences of Archaic period use at this and other sites. In fact, it is somewhat surprising that more Archaic sites have not been found in the canyon. The best explanation for the scarcity of Archaic sites is they are covered by sediments washed into the canyon bottom and are not visible on the surface. Canyon surveys, however, did find 15 sites containing Archaic-style projectile points. Workshop Knoll was the only open, Archaic site excavated and no sample materials (charcoal) for radiocarbon dating were found; consequently, no absolute dates were obtained there.

Although information about the Archaic period in the canyon is quite scarce, the archaeology suggests human presence increased in Clear Creek Canyon during the late Archaic simply because more sites from this period have been found. Small hearths are the only formal remains representing the period and are evidence that Archaic peoples were more mobile; they moved around more than the Fremont. This is not to suggest no houses were being constructed during the Archaic or they only lived in caves. Few Archaic houses have been found in the state, however. A rare example of an Archaic house was encountered near Richfield north

---

[2]The earliest levels at Danger Cave on the Utah-Nevada border near Wendover date to over 10,000 years ago and contain evidence of people hunting essentially modern forms of animals and gathering plants still found in the vicinity of the cave.

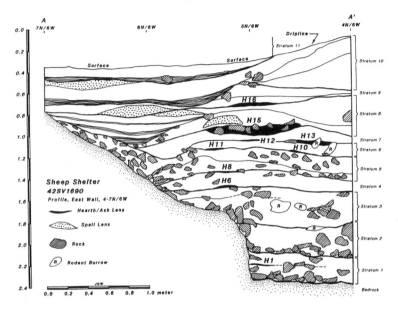

Drawing of Sheep Shelter sediments exposed in excavations
(H = Hearth and its assigned number). Insights into paleoclimates
came primarily from these deposits.

of Clear Creek Canyon. Here a series of hearths, use areas, and a small (about 10 to 12 feet in diameter), shallow pithouse were found dating to about 400 B.C. The house was buried under nearly 6 feet of dirt. In Clear Creek Canyon, late Archaic occupations occurred at both Lott's Farm and Icicle Bench. In both cases the finds consisted of small hearths. The earliest dated to 200 B.C. at Icicle Bench and was nearly three feet below the ground surface. Pithouse 2 at Icicle Bench could also be Archaic since there was no evidence of either ceramics or corn, although it dates to several hundred years later.

As noted, Archaic used only wild foods. At Icicle Bench a grinding stone found in what may have been an early hearth and wild seeds from other features found in backhoe trenches, as well as the early house, point to the importance of plants in the Archaic diet. Deer and mountain sheep bones from the Archaic levels at Sheep Shelter are evidence of the importance of those animals for food. Chipped stone tools and manufacturing debris from Sheep Shelter provide some insights about the production of tools necessary for hunting and processing big game. The archaeological information from Sheep Shelter, as well as from the sites located in open, streamside locations portrays Archaic peoples as more nomadic than the Fremont, moving from place to place depending on seasonal circumstances (see Jennings 1978 in Additional Readings for good descriptions of the Archaic nomadic lifestyle). However, these descriptions are based on a rather limited sample. As noted above, all of the Archaic hearths and other features were deeply buried and very little excavation was focused at that level. It is potentially misleading to assume too much from such a small sample. Perhaps the Archaic peoples did build substantial structures; we simply have not been lucky enough or have not made the effort to find them. The discovery of rather deeply buried houses near Richfield dating to 2,500 years ago is a message to archaeologists that early occupations are present but hidden.

The distinctions between the Archaic nomadic way of life and the more settled Fremont pattern seen later in the canyon begin to blur around 2,000 years ago. The best evidence for these changes in the canyon is Pithouse 2 at Icicle Bench described above. Most likely occupied in the A.D. 400s, this house apparently predated pottery as none was found on the floor; nor was any corn found. However, we know that corn was present in the Sevier Valley by 100 B.C. as corn dated to that time period was found a few miles north of Icicle Bench at the Elsinore Burial site (see Wilde and Newman 1989 in Additional Readings for more on the Elsinore Burial). The absence of corn in Pithouse 2 may be due to many things, but it is also possible that people were not very committed to farming at this time.

Plant remains are an additional data set that help us understand the world people lived in during this important period of transition. Especially useful is pollen collected level by level from deep sites such as Sheep Shelter, Cave of 100 Hands, etc., (see **How Do Scientists Reconstruct Past Climates?** in Chapter 4 on page 64). The pollen analysis done on the project indicates climates shifted to a period of greater moisture at about A.D. 500, a pattern that continued until about A.D. 1150. More moisture means more pine trees on the upper slopes and more marsh-loving plants like cattail and sedges in the stream bottom. It could mean better growing conditions for corn also, provided the summer growing season (the number of frost-free days) was long enough. For corn that usually means about 110 or more days when the nights stay above 32 degrees Fahrenheit.

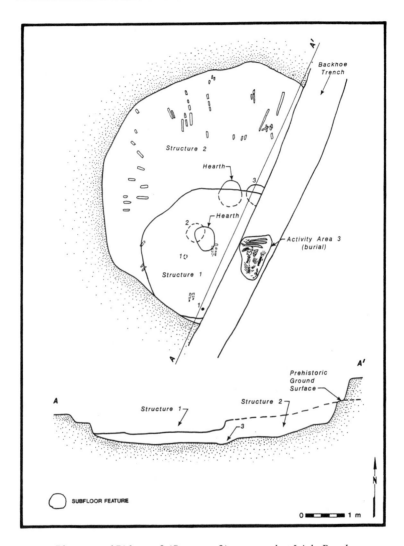

Plan map of Pithouse 2 (Structure 2) excavated at Icicle Bench.
This was the earliest architecture discovered in Clear Creek Canyon.
Structure 1 was built on top of Structure 2 at a later time.

Canyon Rancherias and Villages

The move to farming in Utah appears to have been gradual, occurring over several hundred years (see Janetski 1993 in Additional Readings for more on the gradual shift to farming in Utah). Corn, along with large, subterranean, bell-shaped cists for storage, are present at several places in the state by the end of the first century B.C. Important material changes over the next several hundred years include more elaborate and larger houses, the adoption of the bow and arrow (A.D. 200 or so) and pottery by A.D. 500. Associated with these changes is an emphasis on craft items for personal decoration. Sites found in Utah Valley and the Uinta Basin dating to the early Fremont period (A.D. 1–A.D. 500) contained numerous bone beads as well as some marine shell (*Olivella* and *Dentalium* from the west coast), suggesting an increased emphasis on personal adornment and, by extension, concern with building prestige, social status, and connections with peoples to the west and south.

Between A.D. 500 and A.D. 1000 Fremont life in Clear Creek Canyon centered around small communities, sometimes referred to as rancherias, a term borrowed from the Southwest to describe small Fremont farmsteads encountered throughout the Fremont area. A Fremont rancheria consisted of a pithouse or two and associated granary, and perhaps an outside work area. This description fits the early Fremont occupation at Icicle Bench as well as the much later communities there and at both Lott's Farms and Radford Roost.

By the A.D. 1100s Five Finger Ridge was a popular place to live. Occupation here began with a few houses on the north ridge and expanded fairly rapidly in the early A.D. 1200s. As many as a dozen houses were spread over the top ridges in the first half of that century. An additional 12–18 houses were constructed in the late A.D. 1200s marking the maximum numbers of people at the site and probably the largest population in the canyon (from 60 to 100 people). Based on radiocarbon dates and diagnostic artifacts, especially ceramics and architectural styles, it is likely people were also living at Radford Roost, Lott's Farm, and Icicle Bench during this late thirteenth century population expansion. Additional unexcavated Fremont sites with houses are present in the canyon and could argue for even more people in the area.

The Post-Fremont or Late Prehistoric Period

After A.D. 1350, farming, pithouses, Fremont-style pottery, and other material remains were no longer produced here or elsewhere in the

Fremont area. The canyon was not abandoned, however. The limited data on the post-Fremont era, referred to as the Late Prehistoric, suggest that canyon occupants were few in number (at least when compared to the Fremont era) and they used only wild foods. A different style of pottery, usually referred to as brown ware (as opposed to the Fremont gray wares) and distinctive, basally notched arrow points (called Desert Side-notched) are material evidences of the late period. Information on this era from archaeological investigation comes only from North Cedars Cave, Trail Mountain Shelter and the very sparse remains at Lott's Farm. The scarcity of the remains suggests that Late Prehistoric populations were small and more nomadic, perhaps similar to the Archaic hunter-and-gatherers. However, Late Prehistoric peoples made pottery and farming was practiced to the south in the St. George area; neither pottery nor farming were present during the Archaic.

Some archaeologists have argued that Late Prehistoric peoples were the ancestors of historic Southern Paiute and Ute who were living throughout central, eastern, and southern Utah when the first European explorers came through. Because Fremont farming and artifacts are so different from Late Prehistoric and later Ute and Paiute material goods, others think the Fremont were pushed out of the area to move south and join with the Hopi or other Southwestern farming groups and were replaced by the ancestors of the local Indians. There is some linguistic evidence to support this latter view. This position is opposed by scholars in archaeology who maintain that the change is a response to environmental shifts, not an out-migration. Due to changing conditions, farming became too risky to invest so much effort, they argue, and it was dropped in favor of the always present wild foods. As noted in the introductory section on the Fremont, not all were farmers during the Fremont period; for them this shift would have had little impact.

Whichever explanation is correct, the Fremont style and material trappings disappear by A.D. 1400. After that date the region is occupied by hunters and gatherers about whom very little is known, but whose lifeway appears to have continued until Europeans came into the area.

Historic Period

The valleys of the Sevier River and those along the west facing slopes of the Pavant and Tushar Mountains were peopled by various Ute and Southern Paiute in the A.D. 1700s. Historic accounts of early travels through this region and ethnographic studies suggest the boundary between these two groups is hard to locate, although a line could be drawn from Kanosh to Richfield as the approximate northern boundary of the Southern Paiute people. To the north in Sanpete Valley were the Sanpits Utes while to the west near Fillmore and Delta were the Pahvant Ute. South were the Koosharem, Panquitch, Beaver, and Cedar City bands of the Southern Paiute (see various sections in d'Azevedo 1986 in Additional Readings for more on native peoples of the Great Basin). Linguistic differences were slight between these groups and interaction was likely common. Much of the contact between the Utes (who were often mounted on horses) and the Southern Paiute (who were not) in the late eighteenth and early nineteenth centuries was hostile, with the Utes often raiding the Paiute to capture slaves to trade to the Spanish.

By the 1800s the lives of the indigenous peoples were forever changed by the arrival of Europeans. Disease and displacement by European settlers reduced the numbers of Ute and Southern Paiute dramatically (see Holt 1992 in Additional Readings for more about the history of the Southern Paiute and Smith 1974 for more about the Utes). Small populations of the Southern Paiutes have endured in Koosharem, Richfield, Kanosh, and Cedar City. Many of the Ute people, on the other hand, were assigned to the Uinta Basin on the Uintah and Ouray Reservation in northeastern Utah.

The first European arrivals in central Utah were explorers: the Spanish, and later, mountain men. In October of 1776 the famous Spanish friars, Francisco Atanasio Domínguez and Silvestre Vélez de Escalante passed to the west of Clear Creek on their aborted trip to Monterey, California. The Old Spanish Trail, which connected the Spanish settlement in New Mexico with southern California for several decades in the early 1800s, passed through central Utah. Fifty years after Domínguez and Escalante, mountain man Jedediah Smith journeyed through Clear Creek Canyon on his way to California. These mostly transient travelers foreshadowed the onslaught of migrants of the late 1840s and 1850s. Mormon pioneers moved into the Sevier Valley, established Richfield in 1863, and built Cove Fort to the west in 1867. Joe Lott built his cabin in Clear Creek Canyon in 1877 and was one of the first Europeans to settle permanently here. Although the Lott family stayed in the canyon until 1940, life was not easy. The archaeological excavations at the farm suggest that the family was never prosperous despite the proximity of the Kimberly gold mining operations in the mountains just to the north. Historic farmsteads were not unlike the Fremont rancherias with a house and some outbuildings for storage. Although Clear Creek Canyon has been used for grazing and some farming and recreational hunting and fishing in the last 150 years, historic populations have never been as high as they were in the A.D. 1200s when the Fremont lived here.

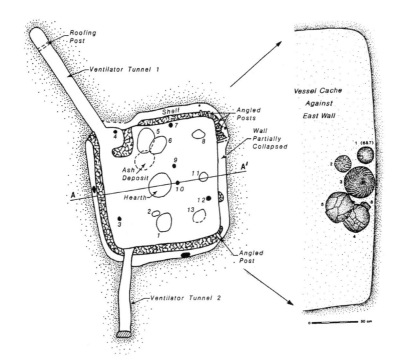

Plan view of Pit Structure 33, Five Finger Ridge.

. . . *we must keep turning the compost heap over and over in order to get a rich, ripe, and aromatic product eventually developed. I think every time (Fremont scholars) fork it all through again, we come nearer to a full understanding, partly because every time it is reforked, some new material is mixed in with the old.*

Jesse D. Jennings (1978)

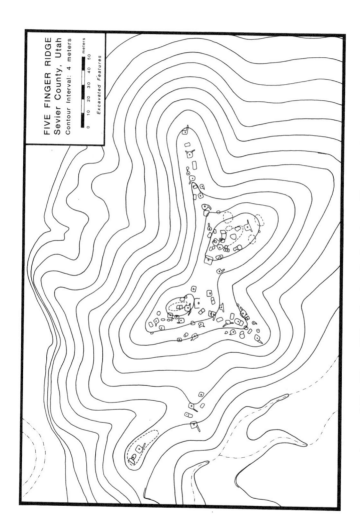

FIVE FINGER RIDGE
Sevier County, Utah

Contour Interval: 4 meters

0 10 20 30 40 50 meters

Excavated Features

A map of Five Finger Ridge showing the locations of homes and granaries. North is to the top of the map.

4
What Was Learned on the Clear Creek Archaeological Project?

Visitors to archaeological projects typically stand at the edge of the work area, watch excavators removing the dirt for awhile, and ask, "What are you finding?" This question stems from the logical assumption that archaeologists are searching for **things**. After all, archaeology is a material science and certainly archaeologists do put all sorts of things into bags and many of those things end up on museum shelves or (in rare cases) on exhibit. However, archaeologists are really after information about the people who left those things behind. A better question to those excavators might be, "What are you finding out?" The offices of archaeologists everywhere are filled with answers (some complete, but many incomplete) to that question, mostly in the form of books and articles. This small book is no exception as it attempts to inform the reader about what the Clear Creek research found out about the lives of peoples in Clear Creek Canyon 500, 1,000, 2,000, and more years ago. By far the most information recovered dated to the Fremont period between 1,000 and 700 years ago.

The following sections discuss some of the materials recovered and attempt to relate what we think they tell us about Fremont life and, to a certain extent, earlier periods. In some cases new data was recovered; in others, the information overlaps or reinforces conclusions of previous research on similar sites around the state. Regardless, as suggested by the insightful quote by the Father of Utah Archaeology, Jesse D. Jennings, the information from this research builds on earlier findings and through comparisons and discussion refines our knowledge about the past.

Past Environments of Clear Creek Canyon

Understanding the natural world of those who lived in Clear Creek Canyon and how that world might have changed or stayed the same was an important goal (see page 64 **How Do Scientists Reconstruct Past Climates?**). The best information to help us understand the natural world are the remains of both animals and plants recovered from excavated sites as well as from contexts away from the sites. The most useful of these data sets are microbotanical remains, or pollen, collected from dirt exposed during archaeological excavations, especially in the caves and rockshelters where soils representing long periods of time were sampled.

People who live close to the land perceive climate change annually. "It was cool and rained a lot last summer." "First frost came later this year." But they farm or schedule hunting or collecting trips according to a more generalized understanding of the climate passed on through oral traditions. Global and regional climate patterns may span hundreds of years or more. Within these general patterns there may be shorter intervals where the patterns are reversed or become more extreme. Plants and animals (including humans) must make adaptations to these changes. Different kinds of plants react differently to climate change according to their physical needs and the opportunities provided them. In their annual reproductive process, plants disperse pollen into the air, which becomes incorporated into the soil. By examining the pollen deposited in the soil, we get hints of what were the most important plants through time. Depending on the span of time between sample intervals, we can see either major or minor vegetation change. Through our understanding of each plant type's growth requirements, we can estimate what the climate must have been like for that particular group of plants for that period of time.

The pollen record from Sheep Shelter spanned a 6,000-year period and documents considerable change in canyon environments during that time. The earliest pollen record, about 5,600 years ago, suggests the climate in the canyon was dry but within a few hundred years became generally warmer and wetter, probably due to summer rains, with increasing amounts of woodland trees like juniper, followed by pines. This period of warmth began to end about 4,000 years ago when winter precipitation increased, temperatures cooled, and summer rains abated, pushing trees upslope. Cool winter temperatures lasted until about 2,800 years ago and were experienced worldwide; this climatic period is generally known as the Neoglacial. During the next 1,000 years plants common to the cool desert shrub environment were abundant in Clear Creek Canyon.

The climate was drier and warmer than during the Neoglacial, but summer rains were probably plentiful because cattails and grasses were well represented in the pollen samples.

Between about 1800–1400 years ago temperatures cooled and precipitation increased. In response to these changes, junipers became more abundant, then pines (mostly pinyon). For approximately the next 400 years pines continued to thrive in the canyon and both cattail and sagebrush became more important up until 950 years ago. Over the next century, there is an abrupt decrease in pines and cattails with a corresponding increase in grass and saltscrub. Other paleoenvironmental records that do a better job of reflecting changes through time suggest this period was characterized by several abrupt changes. For example, tree-ring data from the Sierra Nevadas describe the periods between 1148–1099 years ago as drier than the average, between 1044–995 as warmer and wetter, and between 934–860 years ago as cooler and drier. The implications of these changes for the farming Fremont of Clear Creek Canyon are clear. Domesticated crops would survive during dry periods if irrigated or if summer rainstorms were sufficient. These same crops would thrive during periods of warmer and wetter climates. However, farming was much more risky when conditions were cool and dry since cool weather could shorten the growing period, killing corn and other crops with the first frost.

The last 850 years of the Sheep Shelter pollen record begins with a period of warm and dry weather that may have lasted about 300 years. During this time there was less sagebrush, and grass and pines probably migrated to cooler and moister habitats upslope. The last 500 or so years of the pollen record corresponds to the Little Ice Age. The Little Ice Age was generally a time of cool temperatures and greater than average precipitation, and in Clear Creek Canyon, there was once again abundant pines as well as junipers.

How Do Scientists Reconstruct Past Climates?

Reconstructing past climates was an objective of the Clear Creek Canyon research. All inhabitants, ancient and more recent, were affected by available moisture since the abundance of economically important plants and animals relied on that moisture. A useful tool in reconstructing climatic changes is palynology, the study of plant pollen. Pollens are tough microscopic particles produced by plants during the reproductive process, and different plant families produce pollen with very different shapes. Since the shape of pollen from most plants is known, scientists can discover the kinds of plants that lived in an area by examining the pollen grains. Although a number of factors must be considered (such as size of pollen grains and abundance of pollen produced by different plants), dominance of certain pollen suggests weather conditions that were favorable for the plant that produced it.

Pollen was obtained from samples of dirt from varying levels in trenches exposed during archaeological excavation of Sheep Shelter, which was used on and off for several thousand years.

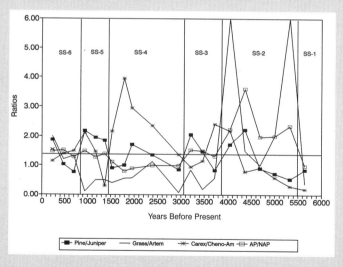

Composite pollen ratios from Sheep Shelter that reflect climate change.

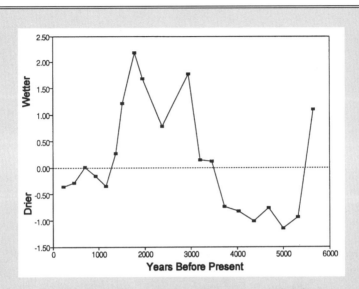

An amplitude curve reflecting paleoenvironmental shifts.

These dirt samples were processed, and the pollen recovered, sorted, and finally, counted. Plant types preferring different climatic conditions were contrasted in terms of ratios. As pollen from plants preferring dry conditions increases over those preferring wet, a change toward drier conditions is suggested. The rather complex figure (opposite) summarizes ratios such as pine (wet) to juniper (dry), grass (summer rain) to sagebrush (*Artemisia*) (winter rain), marsh-loving plants (*Carex*) and plants that flourish in more arid climates (Cheno-Ams) and arboreal (AP) (wet) to nonarboreal (NAP) pollen (drier) from earliest to latest levels at Sheep Shelter. The graph tracks changes in climate above and below the horizontal line representing modern conditions. In general, when the graph goes below the line, it suggests drier conditions, above the line argues that conditions were wetter.

The simple figure (above) attempts to summarize the climate data. The diagram reflects shifts between drier and wetter than today's climate over the past several thousand years.

Fremont Life

Variation and flexibility among the Fremont was so pronounced that a single individual may well have . . . [ranged] . . . from a full-time farmer in a settled village to a full-time hunter-gatherer in the space of a few years.

David Madsen (1989)

The Introduction stated that Fremont refers to a period of time as well as a range of lifeways. The research and excavations in Clear Creek Canyon appear to document Fremont peoples who were committed to farming, although it is not clear how much land was being cultivated. Other strategies less committed to corn farming may have been in place at times during the Fremont period, but it is difficult to identify them. All the sites with houses contained some evidence for domesticated crops. Corn was even found in some of the sheltered sites.

As stated in the Preface, the Clear Creek Project provided one of the few opportunities for archaeologists to assume a regional perspective; that is, to examine closely a number of sites in a defined area (in this case Clear Creek Canyon) so as to compare sites that might be functionally different. Three different kinds of sites were investigated: shelters (caves or rock shelters), remote storehouses or granaries, and villages located along the creek or on ridges. The research suggested that people had used caves and rock shelters in a different way from the large villages.

The small rockshelters may have been used by peoples practicing a more mobile life rather than as temporary stopovers by those living in the valley villages. However, the evidence from the analysis of chipped stone debris and animal bones from the several sites, both villages and rockshelters, suggests that the rockshelters were used primarily as temporary camps for people out on special forays from the villages. This issue continues to be an important focus of research.

Spiritual Life

Concerns with spiritual well-being are and were paramount to Native American peoples in the Great Basin. For that reason, this topic is considered first in the discussion of Fremont life. Discussion of the concept and application of power, shamanism or curing, knowledge of sacred places, the treatment of the dead, oral traditions or stories about life and the natural world, mourning ceremonies, annual dances, and other events related to spiritual life are available in the literature on the religion of Basin peoples (see Conetah 1982 in Additional Readings for a native perspective). The complexities and depth of the spiritual side of the lives of native peoples is neither well understood nor appreciated by nonnatives. Traditional Southern Pauite thought, for example, is similar to that of other Native Americans in that they do not distinguish between the secular and sacred (see Stoffle and Dobyns 1983 for a discussion of this topic).

Despite the importance of spiritual matters in native life, topics such as religion and sacredness are seldom examined by archaeologists. The earlier quote from Madsen, for example, refers to variation in such things as strategies and foodstuffs, not religion or beliefs. It is not that religion is perceived as unimportant by archaeologists; it is simply difficult to identify ideas and philosophies in archaeological debris like bits of pottery and bone, arrowheads, and houses. Archaeology tends to emphasize what it does best: determining the time of site use, describing discarded tools and abandoned houses, and reconstructing diets, among other things. Certainly a reason for the difficulty in sorting spiritual from mundane was presented above: native thought did not separate the secular from the sacred. It may very well be that tangible remains of religious practices are staring archaeologists in the face but are not recognized as such.

When asking questions about ideology, it seems appropriate to wonder whether the religious institutions and belief systems of modern, local, native peoples (who did not raise crops) are similar to those of past farmers like the Fremont; perhaps the beliefs of the Hopi or Colorado River people, such as the Havasupai or Walapai, are more like those of the Fremont farmers. It seems reasonable, however, given the pervasiveness of spiritual concerns in native America, to assume that spirituality was an important aspect of those who lived in the villages and rancherias along Clear Creek.

What remains of religious events or actions? Are there structures, shrines, icons, or other clearly religious features present in Fremont sites? If, as some have suggested, Fremont peoples are ancestral to some Hopi clans, we might expect to find evidence of Puebloan-style, religious features, such as kivas, which are found throughout the area. In fact, early archaeologists interpreted pithouses as kivas. However, Fremont pithouses do not contain the distinctive elements found in kivas such as the sipapu,[1] wall niches where sacred paraphernalia was kept, benches, or

---

[1] A cylindrical pit found in Puebloan kivas that connected religious practitioners with the spirit world.

floor sockets to hold looms for weaving, and this interpretation has now been abandoned. Rock art and figurines may be the most visible remnants of sacred activities. Figurines made of baked clay are easily one of the most distinctive of all Fremont artifacts. They tend to represent people, both men and women, and are highly detailed in some cases and quite abstract in others. Why did people make these figurines? What was their role in Fremont Society? Occasionally, figurines are found in pairs, a man and a woman together, suggesting they could represent courting or fertility. Figurines have also been found in rather elaborate and apparently explicitly structured settings along with miniature pottery vessels, food, and other items. Again, the thoughts that ran through the minds of the people who constructed this setting are difficult to know, although they have been related to a nearby burial.

Despite the extensive excavations at Fremont sites during this project, only a single figurine was found, a small example from Pit Structure 5 at Icicle Bench (see illustration on page 7 in Chapter 1). Although figurines were scarce, rock art is exceptionally abundant in Clear Creek Canyon. Martineau (see Additional Readings) devotes a significant portion of his report on Clear Creek Canyon rock art to offering explanations as to why rock art is sacred. Rock art is sometimes described as doodling or simple depiction of animals and people; however, Martineau denies that such is the case, although he acknowledges that rock art can be highly variable in meaning. He notes native peoples have the utmost respect for rock art and would never think of destroying a rock art panel. The abundant rock art in the canyon may symbolize the importance of the region in the spiritual life of early inhabitants or travelers (see Chapter 5, Clear Canyon Rock Art).

Importantly, archaeology is often affected by the actions of native peoples driven by spiritual motives. On the Clear Creek Project, for example, the potential for the uncontrolled disturbance of burials motivated the Paiute Indian Tribe of Utah to lobby for the complete excavation of Five Finger Ridge so burials would not be destroyed by construction and those found could be carefully removed and reinterred with proper ritual. Ironically, no formal burials were found at Five Finger Ridge.

Social Patterns and Populations

The most important new information to come from the Clear Creek research project has to do with Fremont social life. Community planning and social life has traditionally been a difficult topic to explore through archaeology, since it requires excavation over large areas to be able to see such things as house placement and arrangement, etc. The nearly complete excavation of a large Fremont village (Five Finger Ridge) provided a unique opportunity. For the first time in the history of Fremont research, archaeologists could look at differences in houses (types, locations, and sizes) and material remains (pottery, tools, jewelry, etc.), and variation in construction techniques (pithouses, surface houses, jacal construction, adobe construction) over an entire village. Questions asked focused on whether different statuses existed in Fremont society. In other words, were there social climbers at Five Finger Ridge? How can such questions be answered? One approach might be to look at how living people make status or class distinctions. In industrial societies such as our own, wealthy people mark their position in life by purchasing large houses and filling them with expensive things. Did tribal societies such as the Fremont also mark status differences with valuable material goods? The answer to that is yes, although their definitions of valuables were often different from ours.

Were there differences in material wealth and, therefore, differences in social status in Fremont society? And, to repeat the question asked above, how would we know? Relying on observations of living peoples, if differences in social status existed, we would expect that the majority of houses in a community to be about the same size, since most people are about at the same social level, and a few houses would be considerably larger, marking the residences of those with higher status. In addition, we predicted there should be more "valuable" things in the larger houses than in the smaller houses. The approach used on the project was quite straightforward: look at differences in such things as house sizes and the association of those large houses with valuables. The results of the first part of this exercise were quite clear: some houses were much larger (in terms of amount of floor space) than others. Pithouse 57, for example, located in the heart of the site very near the top of the ridge, was twice as large as the average house and had two cooking hearths (no other house had two hearths). Why would that be so? Perhaps so the owner could make a statement about his wealth and position or to accommodate a larger family (more than one spouse?). Certainly such conclusions are speculative, but the variation in house size demands some explanation.

The second expectation, larger houses should contain more valuable things, was more complicated. To explore this expectation "valuable" had to be defined. Because turquoise and marine shell pendants and beads

had to be imported and all jewelry required considerable effort or investment to make, these items were defined as valuables. The turquoise and
marine shell and finely crafted items such as bone and stone jewelry did
occur more frequently in larger houses, which offered support to this
second expectation. Therefore, the answer to the question "Was there
status differentiation in the Five Finger Ridge community?" has to be a
tentative "yes".

How many people lived at Five Finger Ridge at any one time? An
answer to this question has to come after careful dating of the houses to
determine how many were in use at once since estimates of numbers of
people is based on the numbers of houses (see page 42 **How Long Was
Five Finger Ridge Occupied?** for a discussion of this problem). During
the late A.D. 1200s at least 12 pithouses were in use contemporaneously.
If we assume an average of five individuals per household, about 60
people lived in the village during that period. Considering that Lott's
Farm, perhaps Radford Roost, and the late occupation at Icicle Bench
were contemporary with this era at Five Finger Ridge, the population of
the Fremont community in the canyon may have been close to 100, certainly 75 to 80. These figures are conservative, but suggest that canyon
populations were higher than they are today.

Fremont Village Size

Visitors to Five Finger Ridge were struck by the large numbers of
houses and other constructions at the top of this small knoll. As excavators, we also wondered why this concentration of houses (and presumably
people) occurred here and whether such an aggregation was unusual in
the Fremont area. Many reasons were offered to explain why the large
numbers of houses were placed here on top of the knoll: a better access
to passive solar heat; a stronger breeze; a good view up and down the
canyon; a way to get away from the mosquitos; an easier defense from
enemies, etc. Of course, it is nearly impossible to say with confidence
which of these (or others) might have swayed the original inhabitants to
build here. A search of the archaeological reports on Fremont sites suggests that gathering together in larger communities occurred more often
late in the Fremont period. Certainly, there are numerous small- and
medium-sized villages co-existing with the larger sites (for example the
smaller sites, Icicle Bench and Radford Roost in the canyon, are contemporary with Five Finger Ridge), but the number of places with larger concentrations of people (over 100) appears to increase late in the Fremont
era. Examples included the Parowan Valley, Utah Valley, and Nephi.

Why are there more large sites later in time? It is possible the Fremont were simply increasing in numbers. Although the data necessary to argue this point are scarce, the Clear Creek Project provides some support. For example, it is interesting to note the early dates from the canyon are either from caves or from open sites along the creek. Icicle Bench at the mouth of the canyon was occupied at least 2,000 years ago as was Lott's Farm. Structural sites on ridges (Radford Roost and Five Finger Ridge) are all occupied later; however, people continued to live along the creek at Lott's Farm and Icicle Bench. This pattern of using a wider variety of canyon locales suggests more people were living in the canyon during the later period.

Village Planning and Household Structures

Since Five Finger Ridge was almost completely excavated, archaeologists were interested in looking for evidence of community planning. A map of the site reveals the patterns in the choice of locations for house constructions. Houses are clustered toward the tops of the ridges but, more commonly, just off the crest on the west- or south-facing slopes. Few were on the north facing slope overlooking the creek. Granaries were usually positioned along the ridge crest. Constructing the houses on the slopes required the back walls to be quite deeply incised into the hillside. The walls of the houses were nearly always stabilized with adobe. An unusual kind of home (the excavators called it a secondary pit structure) was also built just off the ridge tops on the ridge slopes. These pit structures were much smaller than the pithouses, measuring about 6 to 8 feet in diameter in contrast with the 20 feet diameter of the larger houses. Analysis of the spatial patterning of the architecture concluded that Fremont households at Five Finger Ridge consisted of a pit structure, a granary, and a secondary pit structure.

The purpose of the pithouses and granaries seems clear—living and storage. The function of the secondary pithouses is more puzzling. Most contained hearths, and metates were found in some, but artifacts and living debris like burned bone were scarce. The very small size precluded use by more than one or perhaps two individuals. It may be that these small structures were sweat lodges or perhaps menstrual or even birthing huts.

An intriguing pattern in the layout of the houses was the three most unusual houses were clustered around a saddle area where the four main ridges joined. These structures included a square, surface adobe house; a jacal structure with no south wall; and a pithouse (Pithouse 57), which was by far the largest of all the houses at the site. Why do all of these houses occur in this area at the top of the ridge? Were there any structures built in the saddle itself? Or could it have served as a central gathering place for the village? Unfortunately, the central saddle area was rather heavily disturbed by heavy equipment when the ridge was being explored for use as highway fill. Nonetheless, careful examination of this area revealed no obvious evidence of additional architecture, suggesting this prime central space was left empty. The apparent absence of houses here argues that this space functioned as a sort of central plaza surrounded by these large, unique constructions. Such an interpretation reinforces the idea that some site planning occurred at Five Finger Ridge.

Use of Household Space

An important research emphasis on the project was investigating how Fremont people used space at the community (village) and household levels. Because of the large spaces exposed and the large number of houses and other constructed facilities excavated at Five Finger Ridge, archaeologists were, for the first time, able to ask questions about use of space with a reasonable expectation of reliable results. The preceding section discussed site planning at Five Finger Ridge. This section presents some conclusions about how people may have arranged activities within houses.

Identification of functionally differentiated space depended on the distribution of artifacts and other debris inside houses. This included small things such as bone fragments, ceramic sherds, and chipped stone debris, as well as larger items such as grinding implements. This kind of analysis is full of potential pitfalls that could lead to erroneous conclusions about activity areas. Houses were not only used for living, they were also used (after being abandoned) as garbage dumps. The potential for the dumped material to be mistaken for debris left in the house by the original occupants is great. Archaeologists refer to artifacts left (and remaining) in place as primary refuse. Artifacts and debris moved or dumped after use are called secondary refuse. To determine whether artifacts were primary or secondary refuse and to begin seeing patterns of household use, the archaeologists point-plotted artifacts that were clearly on the floor and transferred that information to detailed maps of the houses. In addition, the distribution of artifacts on the floor was compared to the distribution of artifacts in the fill immediately above the

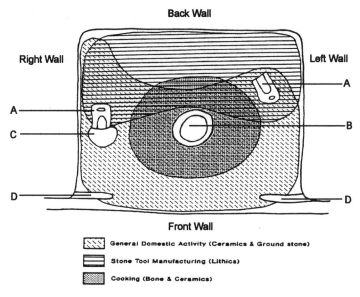

Back Wall

Right Wall

Left Wall

A

A

B

C

D

D

Front Wall

General Domestic Activity (Ceramics & Ground stone)

Stone Tool Manufacturing (Lithics)

Cooking (Bone & Ceramics)

Idealized schematic of Five Finger Ridge pithouse floor artifact distribution;
(a) metate, (b) hearth, (c) catch basin, (d) ventilator shaft.

floors to see if the patterns were different. The assumption was that if
floor and fill distribution patterns matched, the floor pattern was likely
due to dumping and the artifacts were not in primary locations. On the
other hand, if the floor patterns differed from fill patterns and, in fact,
were redundant (similar floor distribution patterns repeated from house
to house), an argument could be made for those materials being primary
refuse and evidence of household activities. Archaeologists were also
aware, because of studies of how living people maintain houses, that the
Fremont most likely periodically swept houses clean, which could leave
little primary refuse from which to infer activity areas. This cleaning
leaves two kinds of debris behind: very small items (flakes of stone and
bone) and large tools such as metates. In this analysis, only larger tools
and debris were used.

Thirty-seven pithouses were discovered and excavated at Five Finger
Ridge. Many of those were on the slopes of the hill resulting in a high
"back" wall and a lower "front" wall where the ventilator shaft(s) entered
the house. The spatial analysis found that general domestic activity (as
evidenced by the presence of grinding stones, ceramics, and bone) was

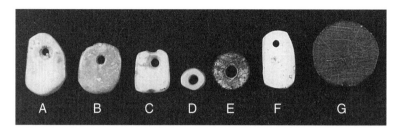

*Turquoise pendants (a–d and f), lignite bead (e), and lignite disk (g)
found at Five Finger Ridge ([g] is about ³⁄₈-inch in diameter).*

more likely to occur in the front of the house and around the hearth,
while stone tool making (marked by the presence of chipped stone
debris and tools) tended to occur in the back of the house. Grinding
implements and associated catch basins for corn or seed flour tended to
be found on either the right or left side of the house. If one can assume
men were more likely to work stone and women were more likely to
cook and use grinding implements, this analysis could be revealing a
division of labor in the house by sex. Interestingly, similar conclusions
were reached by archaeologists at the University of Utah who mapped
very small items on the floor of a Fremont house near Salina, Utah (see
Metcalfe and Heath 1990 in Additional Readings).

These findings are important as they allow us to begin to see social
structure within the Fremont family and to visualize how life's daily
chores may have been carried out in the house. Similar patterns may be
discernible in spaces outside houses where much living would have been
done in the warmer months. At a minimum, the arguments presented here
provide a pattern that may be present in other Fremont houses and can be
sought by future researchers to evaluate the validity of the findings.

Fremont Trade

Trade and economic relations among people is another area that has
long been left unexplored in Fremont studies. The recovery of beads and
pendants of marine shell, turquoise, and other nonlocal minerals from
the Clear Creek sites and from many sites across the Fremont area suggests trade was an integral part of life. Some of the objects, like marine
shell and turquoise, were somehow procured through long-distance connections to the Pacific Coast and to turquoise sources in Nevada, Arizona,
New Mexico, or Colorado. The presence of exotic (from outside the

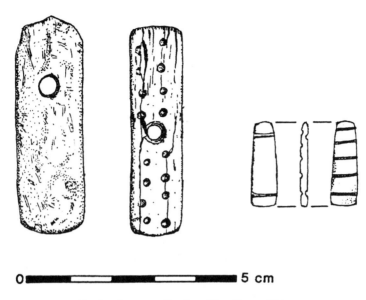

Gaming bones or dice from Five Finger Ridge.

Fremont area) items such as turquoise and marine shell suggested several intriguing questions: Where was the turquoise coming from? How
did the people at the site obtain it? How were the turquoise and other
materials distributed? Were people traveling long distances to obtain
these goods directly or did they obtain these objects from intermedi-
aries? Who was involved in the trading activities? Anyone? Or just a
select few and why did they want them?

In an attempt to answer the first question, analysts sent six turquoise
artifacts to the Brookhaven National Laboratory in New York for specialized chemical analysis (neutron activation). The goal of this analysis was similar to that done on obsidian (see page 82 **Where Did People
Obtain Obsidian?**): to identify the specific chemical characteristics of
each sample and to compare it with the characteristics of various turquoise sources and other turquoise artifacts found in archaeological sites.
Unfortunately, turquoise is more complex chemically than obsidian and
the amounts of certain chemicals vary even within a single source. The
Brookhaven National Lab has amassed a large amount of information on
turquoise samples from the western United States and Mexico and was
able to compare the Clear Creek turquoise to previously analyzed artifacts. Interestingly, the most consistent matches of the turquoise from

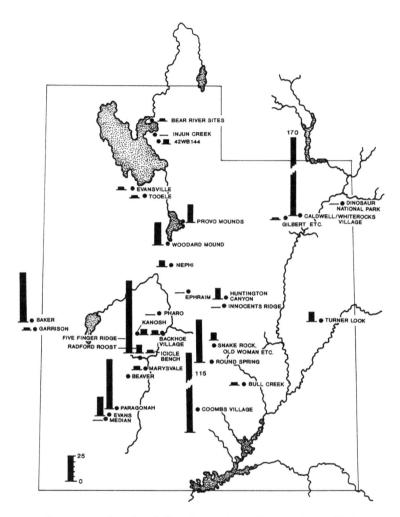

Occurrence of marine shell and turquoise at Fremont sites in Utah.

Five Finger Ridge were with those from Arizona and New Mexico as well as a mine in Nevada. Although the source(s) of the turquoise was not identified, the analysis suggested that the Fremont and the Anasazi were either mining turquoise from the same sources or they were trading with one another.

Local trade, that is, trade among or between Fremont groups, was also important. Specialized analysis of Fremont painted and other pottery recovered from sites in Clear Creek Canyon discovered that a high percentage of those vessels were made in Parowan Valley near Cedar City, Utah. The presence of jet (a very hard form of coal) and other minerals from outside the Clear Creek area, but in Utah, supports the idea of regional trade activities.

How and when did such trade occur? This question is difficult to answer. However, study of descriptions in historic documents of trading patterns that were ongoing at the time of European arrival are helpful. The mountain man rendezvous may be a useful example of what ancient trade events were like. These were very festive affairs with competitive events such as horse and foot racing, feasting, and courting. Of course, gambling and trading also took place. Similar activities were common in the American Southwest during the historic period and provided an important opportunity for trade between the Spanish and numerous Indian groups. These gatherings are often called trade fairs, a name that captures both the economic and social flavor of the gatherings held in favored locations in the west. Trade fairs much like those documented for the Southwest were held prior to European arrival in places like The Dalles, Oregon; Camas Prairie, Idaho; and perhaps in Utah Valley, Utah.

Fremont trade may have occurred under circumstances similar to those at trade fairs. The patterned distribution of nonlocal artifacts (abundant in some areas, scarce in others) could suggest these exotic items were being exchanged during social gatherings held in particular places rather than simply exchanged from hand to hand. Indirect evidence supporting these arguments may be gaming bones. The importance of aboriginal gambling at trading centers such as historic trade forts is well documented in historic accounts and bone dice or gambling counters are one of the most common bone tools at Fremont sites. Could these artifacts, which argue for the importance of gambling in Fremont society, be indirect evidence of regular social and economic gatherings like trade fairs? Certainly annual or even semi-annual festivals with dancing, feasting, and gambling were very important among Great Basin Indians. Perhaps these gatherings have a deeper history than has been documented.

These and other analyses of both local and nonlocal goods recovered from sites in the canyon suggests several things about Fremont trade: (1) both local and long-distance trade were occurring among the Fremont, (2) marine shell and turquoise were moving primarily from south to north, (3) exotic artifacts tend to be more common late in the Fremont period,

Corrugated pitcher
(9 inches high)

Undecorated pitcher
(9 inches high)

What Do Ceramics Tell Us?

Pottery was important to the domestic life of the Fremont in Clear Creek Canyon and elsewhere in Utah. In fact, gray ware pottery is probably the most common artifact found at Fremont sites. This pottery was made by building up the sides with coils and then smoothing the coils with a scraper. The resulting ceramic vessels were often burnished to a soft gloss and well fired. Bowls, jars (with and without handles), pitchers, large storage pots, and even miniature vessels are all part of the Fremont repertoire. Despite the abundance of Fremont pottery no kilns are known. Not all the pottery was plain gray, although it is the most common. A small percentage of vessels, most commonly bowls, were painted (usually a black paint on a white or gray background), some were corrugated, and some were decorated with incised lines, or unique applique sometimes described as "coffee bean." Although red wares were not made by the Fremont, they sometimes rubbed a reddish paint on the vessel exterior.

Interestingly, much of the painted and corrugated pottery was probably not made at Five Finger Ridge or even in Clear Creek Canyon. Analysis of the temper and clay materials used to make the pottery has lead scientists to conclude that many of the black-on-gray bowls and corrugated jars and pitchers found at Clear Creek Canyon sites were made in Parowan Valley many miles to the south and west. Parowan Valley is known for its very large Fremont sites and sophisticated pottery tradition (see Jennings 1978 in Additional Readings for more on Parowan Valley sites such as the Paragonah Site, Median Village, and Evans Mound). How did the people get these Parowan Valley pots? Did they travel there and exchange goods of some kind? The trade fair concept proposed above may help us understand how Fremont trading and exchange occurred, although it is hard to tell whether Clear Creek folks traveled to Parowan Valley or vice versa.

Unusual miniature vessel with coffee-bean applique (2 inches high)

Black-on-white bowl (8.5 inches in diameter)

*Cache of six ceramic vessels discovered in one of the pithouses
at Five Finger Ridge.*

(4) trade may have occurred primarily at regular (annual?) festivals or
trade fairs in certain regions of the eastern Great Basin. These ideas
deserve consideration on future research projects as we try to understand
trade in Fremont society.

Fremont Crafts

The Fremont excelled in the crafts of pottery production and working stone and bone into tools and items of decoration. The artifacts
recovered add to our appreciation of those crafts and give insights about
inter-regional interaction (see page 78 **What Do Ceramics Tell Us?**).

Chipped Stone Tools Were Essential

All pre-European societies in North America relied heavily on stone
for tools and the Fremont were no exception. Chipped stone tools and
manufacturing debris were the most abundant artifacts recovered during
the Clear Creek Project. Stone tools were mostly intended for cutting, bor-
ing, and scraping activities or for use as weapons. Other less distinctive
tools were also clearly important to Fremont people. These are simple,
unaltered flakes that were used once or twice and then discarded. Arrow
points are, of course, the most familiar chipped stone tool and these

Obsidian arrowpoints from the Clear Creek Canyon Archaeological Project.

occurred in a number of shapes and sizes. These artifacts are evidence of the importance of the bow and arrow as a weapon for hunting and perhaps defense. The raw material for chipped stone tools included local volcanic stone, obsidian, and cherts. Obsidian flows are present 30 to 40 miles to the west where raw material is available in abundance (see page 82 **Where Did People Obtain Obsidian?**). An interesting pattern in obsidian occurrence was that obsidian was relatively more abundant in the highland sheltered sites such as North Cedars Cave and Trail Mountain Shelter than in the residential sites in the canyon bottom. It should be mentioned, however, that the percentage of tools made of obsidian remains constant from site to site throughout the canyon; it is the quantity of obsidian debris that decreases in the village sites. Archaeologists are not sure why that is the case.

Bone Tools Take Many Forms

Bone was an important raw material for manufacturing tools, jewelry, gaming pieces, and more puzzling kinds of objects. Most of the bone used came from large animals such as deer or mountain sheep. The multiple uses of the bone from these animals, not to mention hide for leather, is another reason why deer and mountain sheep were important hunting targets.

Where Did People Obtain Obsidian?

Obsidian is a volcanic glass formed when lava cools rather quickly. Like glass, obsidian has no crystalline structure and is readily shaped by flaking. Also like glass, obsidian flakes are very sharp when first struck from a core. These two characteristics made this material highly desirable to peoples who made stone tools, and it was quarried and widely traded wherever in the world it was found. Archaeologists also value obsidian, since the chemical characteristics of obsidian are unique to individual sources. Once sources are known and the obsidian from the sources analyzed, archaeologically recovered obsidians can be traced to specific sources. This knowledge gives archaeologists insights into the movement of obsidian and people across the landscape.

Nearly 100 pieces of obsidian selected from the thousands recovered during the Clear Creek Canyon Archaeological Project were analyzed by BYU scientists using a technique called X-ray fluorescence. The obsidian samples came from the three residential sites as well as Trail Mountain Shelter, Sheep Shelter, and sites surveyed just west of Clear Creek Canyon and they represent obsidians used by Archaic, Fremont, and Late Prehistoric peoples.

The result of the obsidian analysis suggests there was very little change in the obsidian sources being used over several thousand years in the Clear Creek area. About 60 percent of the obsidian analyzed came from the Mineral Mountains and 40 percent was obtained from the Black Rock source from all time periods. Both of these sources are found roughly 30 to 35 miles to the west of the study area. Although only a small percentage of all obsidian recovered was analyzed, these patterns as well as the closeness of obsidian sources for Clear Creek Canyon residents suggests that people were most likely traveling to the sources and quarrying obsidian for personal use.

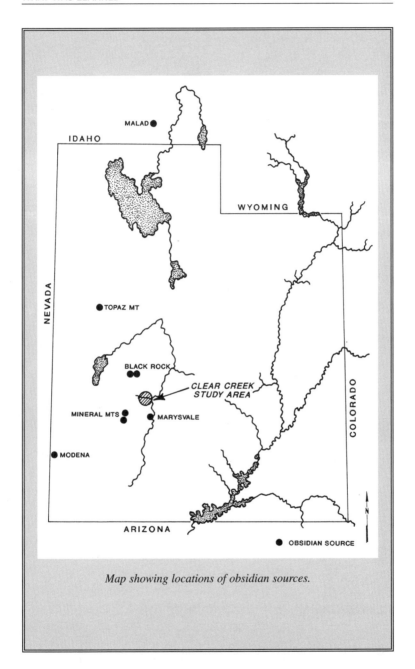

Map showing locations of obsidian sources.

Bone weaving tool(?) (7 inches long)

Hundreds of bone awls were found in the many houses excavated at Five Finger Ridge. It is generally agreed that bone awls were important implements in making baskets and probably clothes. If so, then basketry

production was an important activity at Five Finger Ridge and Radford Roost (where awls were also abundant). The exact process of making tools such as awls is not known since there are no surviving practitioners. It is generally thought, however, that specialized stone tools such as gravers were used for rough carving and splitting the raw bone after which the tools were further shaped with stone rasps.

Bone also provided raw material to make beads, pendants, dice, and a number of tools that defy identification, since their function is not obvious from their shape. Some of these enigmatic tools have been called weaving tools by archaeologists as they somewhat resemble tools used by Pueblo peoples in weaving today. It is possible they were used in making nets, which are known to have been important in rabbit drives for Great Basin Indians. Many questions remain relative to these tools, however. The Clear Creek sites are not unique in producing numerous artifacts of bone; Fremont sites typically contain many bone tools and ornaments.

Ground Stone Uses

Bowl awl

How did the Fremont grind up the hard seeds gathered in the canyon and the corn kernels grown in their gardens? They made grinding tools to crush the hard exteriors of

Manos (all about 7.5 inches long)

these seeds to make them more palatable and digestible. Hard seeds are difficult to chew up so the body can make use of the nutrients and, if not ground, the seeds would most likely pass right through the system with little or no benefit. We are not sure what the Fremont did with the corn or seed flour made from the seeds, but we know Great Basin Indians made mushes flavored with berries or meat with similar flour and these were a very important part of the diet. Grinding tools, therefore, were a valuable part of the everyday equipment in nearly every household.

As one might expect, therefore, grinding stones were a common arti-fact recovered from the sites in the canyon. For the most part, these stone grinding tools took two forms: a large, often troughed stone, called a metate; a smaller handstone or mano that was used to crush the seeds on the metate. Both types were abundant in the residential sites in the canyon. They were commonly made from local sandstones and volcanic rock. Many of these grinding stone were carefully shaped and the surfaces were prepared for grinding by pecking to provide a useful surface to catch and break the seeds. Both metates and manos become very smooth through use, making grind-ing more difficult. The grinding surfaces were regularly revitalized by more pecking on the smoothed facets to make the grinding more efficient. A metate unique to the Fremont is the Utah style, which has a mano rest at one end.

Perishables

Archaeologists only recover a portion of the material culture of any group since many craft items

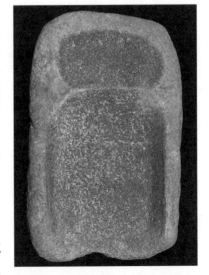

Metate, Utah style (2 feet long)

Chipped stone knife and wooden handle found in a ceramic vessel at Five Finger Ridge (stone knife is nearly 3 inches long).

were made from perishable substances such as wood or plant fibers. Basketry, which most certainly was very important, is only seldom recovered unless the site (and the basket) has been burned or if the site has been kept perfectly wet or dry. Arrow shafts, clubs, hide, fur, feathers, cordage or rope, fire hearths, handles, and many other kinds of tools made with organic materials are lost when sites are subject to repeated wetting and drying. At Five Finger Ridge, remnants of juniper bark matting and wooden tools were discovered in deep deposits that kept artifacts mostly dry over the centuries.

Fremont Foods

> *Although the culture (Fremont) was partly and perhaps predominantly agricultural, the inhabitants of the Fremont region were also dependent in good part on the game supply.*
>
> Noel Morss (1931)

This statement on Fremont diet by Noel Morss is in some ways as applicable today as it was 60 years ago, but more detailed research has refined Morss's general notions considerably. Fremont research at village sites has found time and again that foods used by the Fremont consisted of a mix of wild resources and domesticated plants such as corn, beans, and squash. And such is the case for the residential sites excavated in Clear Creek Canyon. The percentage of mix, that is, crops versus wild foods, varied widely depending on the resources available and the commitment of particular groups to farming.

Recent Fremont research, on the other hand, has shown some peoples relied little on corn and were probably not at all involved with farming.[2] These insights have come from directly analyzing human bone to identify the kinds of foods individuals were eating.

Hunting

Bones from animals are abundant in the Clear Creek sites as are projectile points for hunting and tools for processing the meat. It is no great stretch to conclude hunting was an important activity for the Fremont. Big game animals, such as deer and mountain sheep, were quite important in providing food for the Fremont table, although both cottontails and black-tailed jackrabbits were a consistent menu item, too. The presence of a few bison bones tells us these animals lived in central Utah several centuries ago, but not in great numbers. A few pronghorn bones are also present. Grouse, especially blue, but also ruffed, sage, and sharp-tailed, were also commonly hunted and offered a change in the diet. Smaller animals like pocket gophers and ground squirrels and the occasional muskrat or porcupine were also captured, perhaps by young Fremont hunters. Analysis of the various bone elements represented at the site and the butchering marks on them, argue that hunters often brought whole animals home, including larger game such as deer and mountain sheep. Skinning and butchering appears to have been carried out in the villages.

Although the analysis of the bird bones recovered from the site identified many birds that were hunted for food (grouse and waterfowl), many smaller birds, flickers, jays, blackbirds, and meadow larks, were also identified. Some of these, along with the raptors and owls, were probably collected for their feathers rather than for food. The importance of feathers (or birds generally) is suggested by the discovery of Fremont burials in the Parowan Valley that contained bird remains, suggesting bird skins were attached to garments. Also, archaeologists working in Dinosaur National Park during the 1940s found a headdress decorated with flicker feathers and rock art figures sometimes are portrayed wearing what appears to be feathered headwear. These finds suggest that feathers and bird skins may have been used in a similar way by people living at the Clear Creek sites.

---

[2]The research referred to here was carried out by Steven R. Simms on the many burials eroded from the shores of the Great Salt Lake.

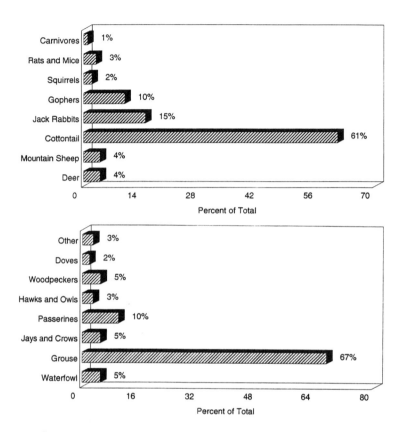

*Percentages of various species represented in the bone scraps found
at Five Finger Ridge: (top) mammals, (bottom) birds.*

It was noted above that big game was important to the Fremont in
Clear Creek Canyon and others have made similar statements about the
role of deer and mountain sheep throughout the Fremont area. However,
a comparison of the animal bone scrap from numerous sites in the state
and from different time periods suggests an interesting trend: Fremont
success at capturing large game animals appears to decrease through
time. These conclusions are preliminary and require considerable more
data, especially from earlier sites; nonetheless, if the trend is verified, it
would argue for long-term population increase during the Fremont period.
The logic of these conclusions is based on the assumption that people
preferred to hunt large game animals rather than small game simply

because more meat was obtained with large game. Hunting large game was, therefore, more efficient. Holding onto that logic, if fewer bones from deer and mountain sheep appear in sites, one can conclude that fewer deer and mountain sheep are available to hunt. On the other hand, ecological explanations are also possible; that is, perhaps some environmental change occurred that resulted in reduced habitat for large game animals. The paleoclimatic reconstructions from Clear Creek Canyon, however, argue for good conditions for big game populations.

Plant Gathering and Crops

Corn was an important food plant in Clear Creek Canyon. Corn remains, including burned and unburned kernels and cob fragments, were common in the samples taken from hearths and floors on Five Finger Ridge, Radford Roost, Lott's Farm, and Icicle Bench. The earliest corn in the canyon was found in Structure 3 at Icicle Bench dating to about A.D. 900. At the Elsinore Burial site a few miles north of Clear Creek, corn cobs found in a deeply buried, bell-shaped pit dated to about 100 B.C. It seems reasonable, then, to assume even though corn was not found in the early house at Icicle Bench, it was present in the area and its absence was most likely due to bad luck. It could also mean people grew corn, but it was not that important yet. However, corn was present in quantities during all time periods at Five Finger Ridge suggesting it was an important food item during the later Fremont period. In the absence of other ways of measuring dependency,[3] it is hard to know how important corn was in the diet. Bean remains were found during later occupations at Icicle Bench and at Lott's Farm. Beans seldom occur in large numbers in archaeological sites and were apparently not as important as corn. No squash seeds were found but remains of cucurbits, a kind of wild gourd related to squash, were recovered at Five Finger Ridge. It is

---

[3]One means of assessing the amount of corn in the diet is through stable carbon isotope studies of human bone. Simply stated, this analysis is based on the fact that different plants assimilate carbon differently during photosynthesis and those differences can be measured through the calculations of ^{12}C to ^{13}C ratios (the two stable isotopes of carbon; ^{14}C is the unstable isotope that decays and makes radiocarbon dating possible). Plants like corn tend to take up more of the heavier isotope (^{13}C); consequently, individuals who eat more corn have a higher ratio of ^{13}C to ^{12}C.

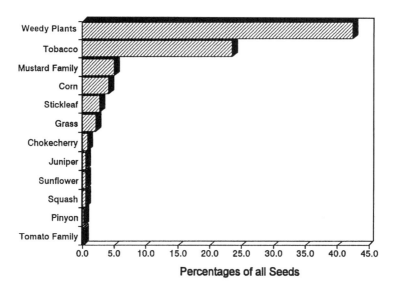

A histogram of the most common plant seeds found at Five Finger Ridge.

possible, of course, that the scarcity of beans and squash is a result of poor preservation or our luck in finding them due to factors of preservation or of sampling. Noel Morss (recall he defined the Fremont in 1931 following his research along the Fremont River) found lots of beans in dry alcove sites in central Utah.

Where did the Fremont grow their corn? Since no evidence of fields or irrigation ditches were found, we can only speculate, but the bottom land along the creek is the most probable spot. Wild plant remains (mostly seeds, but also charcoal) representing food items, medicinal items, and utility wood were common at all sites. Over 50 kinds of wild plants were identified during the study of plant remains found at Five Finger Ridge. The most abundant from presumed food plants are from weedy plants (chenopods): pigweed, goosefoot, and shadscale. These plants produce thousands of very small, hard, black seeds that can be gathered in large quantities. These and similar plants and sunflowers flourish in disturbed soils. Fremont fields undoubtedly encouraged the growth of such plants. Others commonly represented by seeds are coyote tobacco, stickweed, pinyon (nut hulls), tansy mustard, beeweed, knotweed, bulrush, and others in rough order of importance. Coyote tobacco and chenopods occasionally occurred in large numbers suggesting caches.

An interesting pattern discovered during the botanical analysis was abundant cattail pollen on some house floors and on some metates or grinding stones. This discovery is similar to that found at another Fremont site, Backhoe Village at Richfield, Utah. Cattail is abundant in marshy areas along the Sevier River to the east, and, since the pollen and other portions are edible, it may have been an important food item. Certainly the common occurrence of wild plant remains in the Clear Creek Canyon sites and elsewhere is good evidence of their importance in the diet and daily lives of the Fremont.

Summary

The opportunity to explore the early history of Clear Creek Canyon was rare in its scope and the richness of the sites encountered. The regional perspective obtained on the project is especially important as it provided a broader view of how early peoples used this small canyon in central Utah. A portion of the wealth of information (represented by the large quantities of material things from the sites) has been presented in this booklet and in the many volumes reporting the findings in detail. It is virtually impossible to glean all information from such a project as new perspectives and questions are continuously generated by researchers. The artifacts are stored at Fremont Indian State Park and are available for study as are the data representing the observations made by archaeologists. As stated by Jesse D. Jennings at the beginning of the chapter, new information needs to be combined with the old to increase our understanding and appreciation of the past.

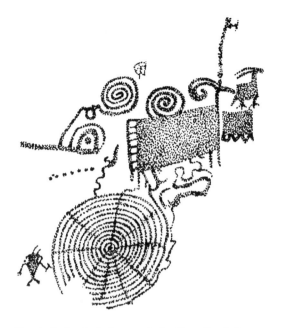

Classic Sevier Style A petroglyph, Clear Creek Canyon.

. . . Clear Creek, a tributary of the Sevier River flowing eastward through a gap between the Tushar Mountains and the Pavant Range, is the type district in which this style (Sevier Style A) occurs.

Polly Schaafsma (1994)

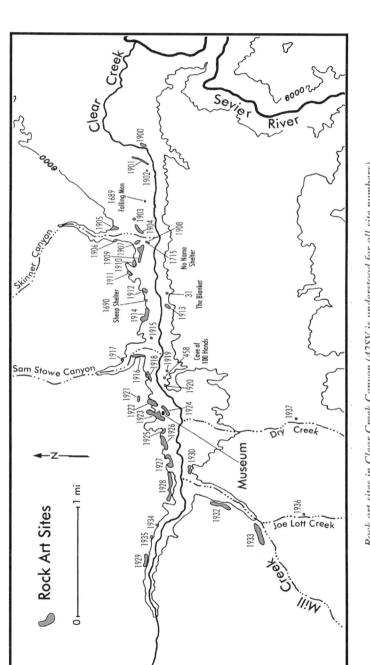

Rock art sites in Clear Creek Canyon (42SV is understood for all site numbers).

5

Clear Creek Canyon Rock Art

Introduction

One cannot stay long in Clear Creek before being struck by the profusion of images drawn on the canyon walls. Mountain sheep and deer troop across sheer cliffs; powerful figures with horn or feather headdresses dominate panels and intimidate viewers; spirals wander in pleasing but illogical patterns. Stare for very long at any panel and less obvious elements, dimmed by wind, rain, and sun, emerge. The abundance of the rock art makes it the dominant visual symbol of past peoples. But, despite the abundance, modern visitors, native or immigrant, struggle with answering the many questions stimulated by the presence of so many images. How long ago were the panels carved here? What does the rock art mean? How many panels are there in the canyon, and why is there so much rock art here? Answering these and other questions is difficult. To begin, we describe how archaeologists document rock art, and then present possible answers to these intriguing questions.

How Was the Rock Art Recorded?

The methods used to record rock art are similar to those used to document all archaeological sites, although greater emphasis is placed on photographs and drawings[1]. At most panels archaeologists could see, in addition to the more obvious elements, bits of paint and faint peckings without clear definition which complicated attempts to describe the ancient panels and made accurate photographic documentation nearly

---

[1]Two different kinds of rock surveys were carried out as part of the Clear Creek research: an interpretive survey directed by the Paiute Indian Tribe of Utah, and a more descriptive survey by Brigham Young University (BYU). The methods used by BYU are those described here.

impossible. Verbal descriptions, therefore, were particularly important to the process of recording the rock art. To capture the most information possible on film, archaeologists took color slides, color prints, and black and white photographs of the panels as well as 8mm video. All photographs included scales to control for size. Some detailed, scaled drawings were made on-site, but many were made in the lab using the photographic record. For example, the video footage was viewed frame by frame on a computer monitor to assist in verifying panel locations and in producing drawings. However, much of the basic information was gathered through detailed verbal descriptions of the specific elements and their spatial relationships within and between panels. All of the above was recorded on special rock art site forms.

To simplify and standardize site documentation as much as possible, descriptions of the rock art used the terms site, area, panel, and element in hierarchical fashion. A **site** was defined as a concentration of rock art with boundaries usually determined by topographic features. Sites could include hundreds or just a few panels. **Area** referred to a smaller grouping of panels within a site, while a **panel** was defined as a discrete rock face containing specific elements. **Element** was the simplest term used and it referred to a discrete item of art such as a circle, a wavy line, a human or animal figure, or some other specific image. All rock art was also described in terms of how the image was made on the rock face; that is, pecked or painted. If pecked, the image is referred to as a petroglyph; if painted, it is a pictograph. In some cases the elements were both pecked and painted.

Important in recording the rock art is recognizing the style of the element or panel. In the absence of other age indicators (see below), archaeologists rely on style as an aid in estimating how old the panels are. Styles defined by researchers who have studied and classified rock art in Utah include: Great Basin Abstract, Sevier Style A or B, Western Utah painted, Historic/Protohistoric Numic (in other words Ute or Pauite), and Historic Euro-American. The majority of the panels could not be assigned to a style and, therefore, could not be affiliated with either a cultural group or a time period but were not considered historic. These were labeled **Unknown Aboriginal**. For example, the many wonderful representations of antlered animals cannot be assigned to a time period.

Great Basin Abstract is considered the earliest style of rock art present in the canyon. It consists mostly of abstract, pecked designs like circles, chains of circles, concentric circles, and curving or meandering lines as well as dots and linear grids. This style likely dates to the

Archaic period in Utah (see Chapter 3 for a discussion of the age of the Archaic period).

Sevier Style A is a classic style assigned to the Fremont period. It was first defined in Clear Creek Canyon by rock art specialist Polly Schaafsma in the 1960s (See *The Rock Art of Utah* in Additional Readings). Sevier Style A consists of neatly pecked human figures wearing necklaces and skirts and with square shoulders and horned heads; mountain sheep figures often in rows; and geometric designs. Western Utah Painted is the pictographic version of Sevier Style A; that is, this style consists of painted (rather than pecked) human or animal figures and geometric designs noted

An example of an Unknown Aboriginal style panel depicting antlered animals (elk or deer).

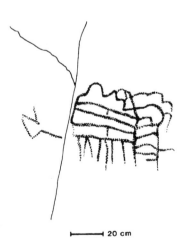

Example of Great Basin Abstract rock art style.

above. It is also considered to be Fremont in age. Importantly, elements stylistically similar to both Sevier Style A and **Western Utah Painted** are found on clay figurines and painted ceramic vessels recovered from houses and other locations dated to the Fremont period. These items provide good evidence that the same people who made the figurines also made the rock art panels. **Sevier Style B** is similar to A but is currently not well defined; consequently, no panels were assigned to this category during the Clear Creek study. Many panels appeared to be stylistically associated with the Fremont culture era but did not

Figures that seem to be holding hands are one example of Western Utah Painted rock art.

fit into one of these defined styles. These were simply referred to as **Fremont**.

Historic/Protohistoric Numic or **Late Historic Ute** styles are the most recent Native American rock art panels. Numic is a linguistic term that subsumes the languages of nearly all native people of Utah and the Great Basin such as Ute, Paiute, and Shoshone. This style includes elements more easily recognized by modern peoples: human figures on horses, human figures with hats, trains, gabled houses, and others (see Sally Cole's book *Legacy on Stone* for more detail on recent aboriginal rock art).

Historic Euro-American rock art also exists in the canyon. These are recent representations left by European settlers since their arrival in the mid-nineteenth century. Panels most often are limited to names or initials along with dates.

How Old is the Rock Art?

The age of the panels can be guesstimated by the kinds of images present. For example, trains and horse-riding figures clearly date to the recent past (after A.D. 1800). Images of individuals carrying or shooting bows and arrows must date to the last 1,800 years or so since prior to that time the dominant weapon was the atlatl. And, logically, the presence of atlatls in rock art panels argues for artists living prior to 1,800 years ago. Another coarse indicator of age is the similarity of some Fremont elements to Anasazi styles to the south. Handprints, which occur at five sites in Clear Creek, are very common in Anasazi rock art. Also, human figures with ducklike feet as well as birdlike feet are present in the canyon and are also found to the south in Anasazi sites. The presence of these elements, then, suggests the sites are contemporary with the Anasazi.

20 cm

Fremont-style (general) petroglyph.

├──────┤ 20 cm

Petroglyph with Historic/Protohistoric Numic elements (train, horse)
and a Historic Euro-American ("RUFUS") element.

Relative dating (whether panels or elements are older or younger than others) is documented by superpositioning, which is simply the placing of an element over an existing figure. Superpositioning of elements in Clear Creek Canyon was noticed by early visitors such as Frank Beckwith from Delta and several instances were documented during the rock art study. In fact, twenty-nine panels exhibited some evidence of superpositioning. In the example above, a historic element (a train) was placed over prehistoric elements (also see discussion of Hunkupp on page 103). Superpositioning is most common at Newspaper Rock, a large concentration of rock art at the confluence of Mill and Clear Creeks. Given the complexity and the abstract nature of many of the panels, it is likely more examples of superpositioning were present but not clearly evident to the archaeologists.

Direct dating of rock art has been attempted by dating lichens that have grown over the panels, by scratching organic matter from the painted elements and dating the material by small-sample radiocarbon methods,

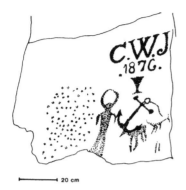

|← 20 cm

Good example of Historic Euro-American style over prehistoric elements.

and by dating the oxided patina or desert varnish surface that has formed since panels were pecked or painted onto the cliff face. None of the these techniques were attempted on the Clear Creek study.

How Much Rock Art is There?

How much rock art is there in the canyon? Archaeologists recorded 43 sites containing 697 panels and well over 3,000 elements in the area examined (see map at the beginning of the chapter on page 94). That area stretched from about two miles west or upstream from the junction of Clear and Mill Creeks to the mouth of the canyon, a distance of about five linear miles. The majority of the sites found were in the main canyon, although some panels occur in side drainages. Certainly more rock art might be present in areas not looked at, and surveyors might have missed some panels. Nonetheless, these numbers convey the notion that rock art is abundant in Clear Creek Canyon. The quantity of rock art, including numbers for panels/elements assigned to each style mentioned earlier, is presented in the short table on page 102. Sevier Style A was the most common with 1,194 elements. When these numbers are combined with Western Utah Painted and general Fremont, there are 1,593 panels that were likely placed in the canyon during the Fremont era. By far the majority of the rock art consists of petroglyphs (87 percent).

A simple answer to why there is so much rock art along Clear Creek could be that the canyon stone was attractive to ancient artisans. The stone is a cream-colored, welded tuff (volcanic ash and rock fragments) that slowly browns through time. Pecking through the darker surface starkly contrasts with the underlying light layer making the rock an excellent medium for rock art. Paints used were nearly always a dark red made from clays or stone with a high iron content and contrast less well with the rock, which could also explain why painted panels are less common than pecked.

Some interesting patterns are present in the distribution of rock art. For example, most panels occur on the north side of the canyon. Of the

Rock art panel known as Newspaper Rock at the mouth of Mill Creek in Clear Creek Canyon.

20 cm

Frequency of Style Occurrences

Rock Art Styles	No. of Elements	% of Elements	No. of Panels*	% of Panels	No. of Sites*	% of Sites
Sevier Style A	1,194	32	70	10	19	44
Western Utah Painted	108	3	25	4	13	30
Great Basin Abstract	162	4	21	3	11	26
Fremont (General)	261	7	59	9	19	44
Unknown Aboriginal	1,870	49	461	68	39	91
Historic (Euro-American)	142	4	52	8	11	26
Historic (Ute)	38	<1	7	1	1	2

*Some panels and sites are counted twice.

43 sites recorded, 31 are on the north. The sites on the south side are not only fewer in number, they are also smaller, accounting for only 12 percent of the panels. This pattern could be used to argue that much rock art was drawn/pecked in the winter when the cliff faces were warmed by the winter sun and were pleasant places to spend some time being creative. On the other hand, more cliff face is available on the north side and the steep, loose talus slopes common to the south side of the creek, may have made access to appropriate cliff faces more difficult. Another pattern in distribution is the tendency for rock art to be more abundant closer to the village sites. For example, nearly three quarters of all rock art occurs within a mile radius of Five Finger Ridge, the largest site in the canyon. This could suggest much of the rock art was created by members of the Five Finger Ridge community.

What Does the Rock Art Mean?

Is rock art a form of writing? Are the panels enigmatic messages? Are they maps? Do they record real or fictive events? These questions are very difficult to answer in the absence of the artists who left the panels for us to ponder. Few archaeologists would argue that rock art represents a formal writing system, but most recognize these images are visual expressions of thoughts and ideas and are, in that sense, a form of communication. What those ancient ideas were or what the artisans were trying to make known is a fascinating question. Common interpretations include some notions of shamanism related to hunting magic. That is, the horned figures may represent influential leaders who directed important hunting activities. These interpretations are given credibility by the presence of so many sheep and deer figures, which, of course, represent desirable game animals. In fact, several specialists have argued Fremont rock art is commonly found in places that would have been good hunting grounds rather than choice places to live (see discussion in *Rock Art of Utah* by Polly Schaafsma). Actually both may have been true in Clear Creek Canyon. That is, we have already pointed out that rock art is more common near the village sites, but the canyon may have also been good hunting grounds for mountain sheep and deer in the past. The canyon is still a wintering ground for deer. In Nine Mile Canyon, a renowned rock art region in eastern Utah, panels are typically located near canyon confluences and many clearly depict hunting activities. This pattern is also true in Clear Creek. One of the largest panels previously mentioned, Newspaper Rock, lies at the confluence of Mill and Clear Creeks. Insights of the artists into animal behavior are also clear in some panels as has been pointed out by Ray Matheny of BYU who has done considerable research in Nine Mile Canyon. Depictions of mountain sheep show lambs following ewes and rams traveling in groups (both of which are characteristic behavioral patterns for mountain sheep) have been documented in Nine Mile Canyon and some are present in Clear Creek.

Other rock art scholars emphasize the religious aspect of the panels. The tendency for the dominant figures in panels to wear elaborate headdresses, jewelry, have facial decoration, and carry various kinds of paraphernalia could suggest some kind of ritual activity. LaVan Martineau (see Additional Readings) emphasizes religion and incorporates Hopi beliefs into his interpretation of a number of the panels. Martineau argues that the panels are visual images of origin stories, migrations, cultural relationships (between the Anasazi and Fremont, for example), ceremonial activities, traditional food getting activities (pinyon harvesting, for example), as well as representations of the natural landscape.

Several of the Late Historic Ute panels can apparently be traced to a real historic event. According to local tradition, at least one such panel (found at site 42SV1928) was created in the 1870s by Hunkupp, a Ute from Kanosh, Utah. He had recently made a trip to the east by rail and pecked this panel during his return trip to his home to the west and north of Clear Creek Canyon. Not only does this panel show trains and European-style houses, it also is an example of superpositioning as several Fremont-style elements are present behind the historic artwork.

*Panel attributed in part to Hunkupp, a Ute Indian from Kanosh, Utah,
who reportedly pecked the trains on the rockface during his return
from a trip back east.*

Five other panels at the same site also show trains and gabled houses. It
isn't clear whether all can be attributed to Hunkupp or if others simply
copied the original.

Summary

This short chapter can only serve to draw visitors' attention to the
rock art in the canyon. Drawings and words, even photos, do not do jus-
tice to this extensive ancient gallery. To appreciate the rock art completely, one must see it. Visitors are encouraged to walk the paths
through the park and enjoy the panels first hand. Each can then ponder
the thoughts that might have been on the mind of the maker, or at least,
draw personal conclusions as to their meaning. Detailed descriptions of
all rock art sites are presented in Volume Two, Parts 1 and 2, of the Clear
Creek Canyon Archaeological Reports (see Additional Readings).

Restored black-on-white bowl from Five Finger Ridge.

The archaeological resources of the state have not been and are not being adequately protected. The present writer failed to visit one locality where the archaeological material had not been disturbed in one way or another. In some cases, the site had even been dynamited and the scraper used on them in the attempt to get "Indian relics." It should be stated in this connection that the common "man of the street" or laymen were not alone in destroying these valuable archaeological specimens, but school teachers and principles (sic) even have participated in the wholesale destruction of sites.

An educational program should be undertaken to acquaint the public with rules and regulations governing archaeological resources of the state.

Elmer Smith (1937)

Fremont Indian State Park with the remaining portion of Five Finger Ridge visible across Interstate 15.

6

Archaeology and the Public

The Clear Creek Canyon Archaeological Project is a wonderful illustration of the importance of public involvement in archaeology. Project directors and sponsors were committed to inviting the public to see archaeologists at work and giving those interested the chance to view an excavation and the kinds of challenges it presents as well as the kinds of things and information recovered. Local schools bussed students to the project to watch the excavations and to question the archaeologists. The many opportunities for interaction between the research team on-site and the public resulted in a better understanding of why cultural resources such as these need to be protected from vandalism and investigated in advance of ground-disturbing activities such as road building.

The payoff for these efforts was, in this case, well beyond expectations. The discovery of Five Finger Ridge was a direct consequence of public involvement. The recognition of the enormity of that site and the excitement deriving from the research there led indirectly to the expansion of the research to include more survey and test excavations in the uplands, the expansion of the rock art research to include an interpretive survey by the Paiute Indian Tribe of Utah, and, ultimately the establishment of Fremont Indian State Park and Museum as a place to see the results of the archaeology and learn the history of the canyon.

Public interest in archaeology in Utah and the United States generally has grown dramatically during the past decade. The growth of the many chapters of the Utah Statewide Archaeological Society (USAS) has been tremendous. At least 12 chapters with a total membership between 300 and 400 now exist in the state. That growth has been due to many factors, but, in part, it is a result of the realization by the professional archaeological community that archaeology needs to be accessible to the public. Numerous Utah professionals spend many volunteer hours as sponsors or advisors to the USAS chapters. And their time is

Local school children visiting Icicle Bench during excavation.

well rewarded. USAS members likewise donate thousands of hours working on their own or with professionals on research projects or in other ways on behalf of archaeology. A further expression of those interests is the growth and response to Archaeology Week celebrations across the United States. In Utah, Archaeology Week has been broadened to Heritage Week to include paleontology and history. Many local activities occur each spring across the state to inform and involve the public further in these fascinating sciences. Collaboration between professionals (represented by the Utah Professional Archaeological Council [UPAC]) and USAS is best exemplified by the joint sponsorship of Utah Archaeology, a journal dedicated to distributing information about local archaeological research.

One impact of public involvement in archaeology has been the reduction in the numbers of archaeological sites being looted. As early as the 1930s, professional archaeologists recognized the destruction of sites by the curious public had to somehow be slowed or the unwritten history of native peoples would be irretrievably lost. Writing in 1937, Elmer Smith of the University of Utah was alarmed at the number of sites being dynamited or destroyed by "the scraper" to obtain "Indian relics" (see above quote). What was particularly surprising to him was professional people such as school teachers were participating in the destruction. Smith went on to propose the implementation of an educational program "to acquaint the public with rules and regulations governing archaeological resources of the state." Smith's recommendations were not pursued. Only recently have such programs been developed, and it has taken the combined efforts of federal and state agencies, as well as public and private universities to put them in place. Those efforts continue.

An important factor in the current success of public archaeology has been the hands-on involvement of avocationalists in field work. Many avocationalists are well-read on archaeological topics (due in part to the statewide certification program) and have years of experience in recognizing artifacts and cultural remains. They make up a largely self-taught, yet very knowledgeable and very reliable labor force. Many research projects have been completed because of their valuable contributions. An equally valuable contribution is the assistance the avocational public have provided in the very difficult task of protecting the irreplaceable archaeological record through site stewardship and informal education.

What Are the Laws that Protect Archaeological Sites?

Cultural resources (this includes historic buildings as well archaeological sites) have been recognized as valuable by the federal and state governments for nearly a century. In 1906 the federal government passed the first legislation to protect antiquities on federal lands. The majority of the laws that protect archaeological sites were written and passed during the 1960s and 1970s and represent a shift in public policy toward more of a stewardship role. Lobbying by the Society for American Archaeology and by many avocational organizations across the United States was instrumental in passing much of this legislation which also established "Cultural Resource Management" as a legitimate concern. This legislation lead ultimately to the proliferation of private archaeological contracting firms to assist the various federal land-managing agencies in complying with these new laws. The amount of archaeological work done beginning in the 1970s and continuing to the present has flooded the professional archaeological community and the interested public with new information about the past.

Federal Legislation
Antiquities Act of 1906

Provided for the protection of antiquities on federal lands and gave powers to the president to set aside lands with demonstrated scientific, historical, or prehistoric values. President Bill Clinton used this law when he set aside the Grand Staircase-Escalante National Monument.

Reservoir Salvage Act of 1960

This important act required that archaeological survey be done in advance of federally funded or sponsored reservoir projects such as the Glen Canyon Dam project in southern Utah. The law also mandated that federal agencies planning such projects contact the Secretary of the Interior about those plans in advance of construction.

National Environmental Policy Act of 1969

This act required that all federal agencies identify ways to insure that environmental values are given weight in making project decisions. The law required that an environmental impact statement be drafted for any federal actions that might affect the environment.

Executive Order No. 11,593

This very important order issued in 1971 required that all executive branch agencies (Bureau of Land Management, U.S. Forest Service) (1) compile an inventory of the cultural resources on their lands, (2) nominate eligible sites to the National Register of Historic Places, (3) preserve and protect their cultural resources, (4) aid in preserving and protecting nonfederal cultural resources.

Archaeological Resources Protection Act of 1979

The Archaeological Resources Protection Act of 1979 gave teeth to the Antiquities Act of 1906 by providing for stricter controls over federally owned sites and heavier penalties for vandalism of archaeological sites.

Native American Grave Protection and Repatriation Act of 1990

This law, referred to as Public Law 101-601 or by its acronym, NAGPRA, protects Native American burial sites on federal lands and regulates the removal of human remains, burial objects, sacred objects, and objects of cultural patrimony. It also identifies a process for the return of human remains and certain cultural objects, upon request, to federally recognized Native American tribes. NAGPRA is momentous as it returns significant control to Native American peoples over their own heritage and the material remains of that heritage.

Utah State Legislation

Antiquities Act of 1973

Established the Antiquities Section and the position of State Archaeologist within the Utah Division of State History and identified procedures to protect archaeological and paleontological sites on state lands including penalties for vandalism. This act has been amended a number of times but the essence of the law is intact.

Antiquities Protection Act of 1992, Utah Native American Grave Protection and Repatriation Act

This legislation parallels in many ways Public Law 101-601 by determining the rights of Native American to certain Native American human remains and objects with which they are affiliated. This bill expanded NAGPRA by extending the concerns and protection expressed in the federal law to state lands. The bill does not pertain to finds prior to March 1992.

Utah Statewide Archaeological Society

Those who are interested in being involved in archaeology, whether it be in the field or in museums, can pursue that interest by joining one of the many local chapters of the Utah Statewide Archaeological Society. To assist interested parties in that involvement, each current USAS chapter is listed along with the geographical area it serves.

- Alkidaa, Sanpete Valley
- Castle Valley, Price area
- Central Utah, Richfield
- Dixie/Jennifer Jack, St. George
- Iron County, Cedar City
- Moab Archaeological Society, Moab
- Promontory/Tubuduka, Ogden
- Salt Lake/Davis, Salt Lake and Bountiful
- Trail of the Ancients, Blanding area
- Uintah Basin, Uintah Basin
- Utah County, Utah Valley
- West Desert, Fillmore

Additional Readings

Clear Creek Canyon Archaeological Project Reports[1]

Baker, Shane A., and Scott E. Billat
  1994   *Clear Creek Canyon Archaeological Project Volume Two: Rock Art; Part 1: Report.* Museum of Peoples and Cultures Technical Series No. 92-17. Brigham Young University, Provo.

Baker, Shane A., and Scott E. Billat
  1994   *Clear Creek Canyon Archaeological Project Volume Two: Rock Art; Part 2: Panel Drawings.* Museum of Peoples and Cultures Technical Series No. 92-17. Brigham Young University, Provo.

Janetski, Joel C., Richard K. Talbot, Deborah E. Newman, Lane D. Richens, and James D. Wilde
  1997   *Clear Creek Canyon Archaeological Project Volume Five: Results and Synthesis.* Museum of Peoples and Cultures Technical Series No. 95-9. Brigham Young University, Provo.

Talbot, Richard K., Lane D. Richens, James D. Wilde, Joel C. Janetski, and Deborah E. Newman
  1997   *Clear Creek Canyon Archaeological Project Volume Four, Part 1: Icicle Bench; Part 2: Radford Roost and Lott's Farm.* Museum of Peoples and Cultures Technical Series No. 94-25. Brigham Young University, Provo.

Talbot, Richard K., Lane D. Richens, James D. Wilde, Joel C. Janetski, and Deborah E. Newman
  1997   *Clear Creek Canyon Archaeological Project Volume Four, Part 3: Five Finger Ridge.* Museum of Peoples and Cultures Technical Series No. 95-8. Brigham Young University, Provo.

---

[1]These are draft reports submitted to the Utah Department of Transportation. Final publications are planned for the Occasional Papers Series of the Museum of Peoples and Cultures at Brigham Young University.

Wilde, James D., Richard K. Talbot, Lane D. Richens, Deborah E. Newman, Joel C. Janetski, and Shane Baker

    1997   *Clear Creek Canyon Archaeological Project Volume Three: Surveys and Small Site Tests.* Museum of Peoples and Cultures Technical Series No. 91-10. Brigham Young University, Provo.

Wilde, James D., Richard K. Talbot, and Joel C. Janetski (editors)

    1994   *Clear Creek Canyon Archaeological Project Volume One: Introduction and Background.* Museum of Peoples and Cultures Technical Series No. 91-10. Brigham Young University, Provo.

Others

Beckwith, Frank

    1947   *Millard and Nearby.* Art City Publishing, Springville, Utah.

Cole, Sally J.

    1990   *Legacy on Stone: Rock Art of the Colorado Plateau and Four Corners Region.* Johnson Books, Boulder, Colorado.

Conetah, Fred A.

    1982   *A History of the Northern Ute People.* Edited by Kathryn L. MacKay and Floyd A. O'Neil. Uintah-Ouray Ute Tribe, Salt Lake City.

d'Azevedo, Warren L. (editor)

    1986   *Great Basin.* Handbook of North American Indians, vol. 11. William C. Sturtevant, general editor. Smithsonian Institution, Washington, D.C.

Hawkins, Bruce, and Lorraine Dobra

    1982   *Archaeological Excavations at the Lott's Farm Site.* Ms. on file, Antiquities Section, Utah Division of State History, Salt Lake City.

Hogan, Patrick, and Lynne Sebastian

    1980   *The Variants of the Fremont: A Methodological Evaluation.* In *Fremont Perspectives,* edited by D. B. Madsen, pp. 13–16. Antiquities Section Selected Papers Vol. VII, No. 16. Utah State Historical Society, Salt Lake City.

Holt, Ron

    1992   *Beneath These Red Cliffs: An Ethnohistory of the Southern Paiute.* University of New Mexico Press, Albuquerque.

Janetski, Joel C.

    1993   The Archaic to Formative Transition North of the Anasazi: A Basketmaker Perspective. In *Anasazi Basketmaker, Papers from the 1990 Wetherill-Grand Gulch Symposium,* edited by V. Atkins, pp. 223–241. Cultural Resource Series No. 24. Bureau of Land Management, Salt Lake City.

Jennings, Jesse D.

    1978   *The Prehistory of Utah and the Eastern Great Basin.* Anthropological Papers No. 98. University of Utah Press, Salt Lake City.

Judd, Neil M.
    1926   *Archaeological Observations North of the Rio Grande.* Bulletin No. 82.
        Bureau of American Ethnology, Smithsonian Institution, Washington, D.C.

Larsen, Vonn
    1990   A Fluted Point from Clear Creek Canyon, Utah. *Utah Archaeology* 1990
        3:133–136.

Madsen, David B.
    1989   *Exploring the Fremont.* Utah Museum of Natural History Occasional Paper
        No. 8. University of Utah Press, Salt Lake City.

Martineau, La Van
    1985   *The Clear Creek Project.* The Paiute Indian Tribe of Utah, Cedar City.

Metcalfe, Duncan, and Kathleen M. Heath
    1990   Microrefuse and Site Structure: The Hearths and Floors of the Heartbreak
        Hotel. *American Antiquity* 55:781–796.

Montgomery, Henry
    1894   Prehistoric Man in Utah. *The Archaeologist* 2(8):340.

Morss, Noel
    1931   *The Ancient Culture of the Fremont River in Utah.* Papers of the Peabody
        Museum of American Archaeology and Ethnology, Vol. XII, No. 2. Harvard
        University, Cambridge.

Schaafsma, Polly
    1994   *The Rock Art of Utah.* Reprinted. University of Utah Press, Salt Lake City.
        Originally published 1971, Papers of the Peabody Museum of Archaeology
        and Ethnology Vol. 65. Harvard University, Cambridge.

Smith, Anne M.
    1974   *Ethnography of the Northern Utes.* Papers in Anthropology No. 17. Museum
        of New Mexico Press, Albuquerque.

Smith, Elmer R.
    1937   *Archaeological Resources of Utah.* Ms. on file, Department of Anthropology,
        University of Utah, Salt Lake City.

Stoffle, Richard W., and Henry F. Dobyns
    1983   *Nuvagantu: Nevada Indians Comment on the Intermountain Power Project.*
        Cultural Resource Series No. 7. Bureau of Land Management, Reno, Nevada.

Wilde, James D., and Deborah E. Newman
    1989   Late Archaic Corn in the Eastern Great Basin. *American Anthropologist* 91:
        712–720.